TORAH with Love

A Guide
for Strengthening
Jewish Values
Within the Family

DAVID EPSTEIN
SUZANNE STUTMAN

Foreword by Elie Wiesel

PRENTICE HALL PRESS · NEW YORK

Dedicated, with love, to our families.
With them we share food
and words of Torah at the table.

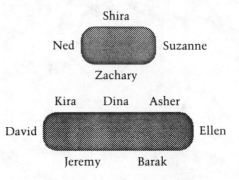

Shira

Ned   Suzanne

Zachary

Kira   Dina   Asher

David   Ellen

Jeremy   Barak

Published by Prentice Hall Press
A Division of Simon & Schuster, Inc.
Gulf + Western Building
One Gulf + Western Plaza
New York, NY   10023

PRENTICE HALL PRESS is a trademark of Simon & Schuster, Inc.

Library of Congress Cataloging-in-Publication Data

Epstein, David, 1935–
Torah with love.

1. Bible. O.T. Pentateuch — Study and teaching
(Primary) 2. Judaism — Study and teaching (Primary)
I. Stutman, Suzanne.   II. Title.
BS1227.E67   1986   296.7'4   85-28107
ISBN 0-13-925371-8

Designed by Irving Perkins Associates

Manufactured in the United States of America

1 2 3 4 5 6 7 8 9 10

Contents

Foreword

I speak about Torah with passion—above all with passion. Study was our first passion and has remained our constant obsession. My first memory is not as a child in kindergarten but as a boy in *heder*. I remember my first teacher and the first lesson. I remember through them my encounters with Adam and Eve, but not with the serpent. I even remember their children and the way they received temporary quarters in the commentaries of Rashi. I remember the sensation that took hold of me when I first opened an old tractate of the Talmud. I was seized with an expectation and a hope that are with me still.

What do we find in these books? Ideas, yes. Stories, yes. Words, naturally. But now we know after studying that they contain an unknown world full of mystery, wonder, and courage. We chose language over violence, history over geography, time over space, imagination over reality. Away from Jerusalem we lived in Jerusalem. In exile we found the way to worship in the Temple. How did we do it? We closed our eyes, and we let the past dominate the present through the words we read in the Book of Moses, and then we taught them.

Unlike other traditions and civilizations, Judaism is not a heritage offered by the dead to the living: it is a heritage offered by the living to the living.

Elie Wiesel

Preface

The Smithsonian Institution has an exhibit to show how even the most modest manufactured product cannot be created by one person in one place. An ordinary yellow No. 2 pencil is shown at each stage of production. Each ingredient is created and transported from different parts of the world. The wood, lead, rubber, metal fastener for the eraser, paint, and glue all involve separate industries and complex machinery which in turn have their own subset of component industries for mining, growing, manufacturing and transporting.

This book on family Torah study is not merely the product of two minds sitting in front of a computer. Rather, the writing is the result of countless diverse influences that bring us to the present stage. Among the immediate influences are several persons whose involvement must be mentioned:

J. Michael Stern of Washington, D.C., started family Torah discussions with his children 15 years ago. His intellectual powers and his achievements through independent scholarship are beyond the grasp of most of us. His example, however, is within the reach of all of us. He encouraged and motivated each of us and other families to start talking Torah within the family.

Our immediate inspirations were our families, which did not know (nor did we) that they were the testing grounds of an idea that would come to fruition in this book.

Ellen Epstein radiates the intense warmth which permeates the family. In addition to the obvious family responsibilities, she has also authored several books and is a working oral historian whose purpose is to assist families to preserve their past.

Ned Stutman cannot be defined by his multiplicity of professions: attorney, photographer, Torah reader, philosopher, and soccer coach. His work as an attorney on behalf of the handicapped is but one manifestation of his limitless ability to give of himself to a larger community. His role in keeping the family glued together was never more evident than during the writing of this book.

Among those directly involved in the production of the book, we express boundless gratitude to Linda Purdy, who was involved in many administrative responsibilities. Technical assistance was provided by Saul Singer and Elizabeth Shanks. Mary Kennan and Marlys Lehmann of Prentice Hall Press each provided valuable editing suggestions.

Rabbi Jacob Halpern of the Washington Board of Jewish Education gave encouragement and made valuable suggestions. Joshua Rokach of Washington, D.C., made some acute observations.

A general influence on each of us is Rabbi Arthur Bogner of Washington, D.C., who has led us into ever deeper studies of the tradition.

David Epstein
Suzanne Stutman

Washington, D.C.
5746 | 1986

Introduction

WHY WE ARE MEETING

The impulse to open a book is not a chance occurrence. When browsing in a bookstore or library, you may skip over books on raising zebras, repairing thrusters on space shuttles, or reading tea leaves. Your eye catches the title of this book and suggests an idea you have been vaguely thinking about ever since your child began to talk. The title may also remind you of a conversation with an acquaintance that caused some stirrings within you.

Knowing something about the authors and why this book was written may give you a better idea of its value to you and your family. As is obvious, the book is co-written, every word having been considered by both of us.

For these comments, each of us will write separately.

Comments of David Epstein

If asked what I do, I answer that I am a trial lawyer who is regularly involved in trials in courts across the country. My experience in the exciting, highly competitive world of the courtroom has no obvious bearing on writing a book about teaching values to a family through the Torah. Yet, I have attempted to place in this book some of the drama that does, from time to time, surface in a courtroom. The excitement for a lawyer of participating in a trial is the opportunity to be the director, author, and actor in a drama involving real people where something of value is at stake. The issue in the criminal case is whether an individual should lose freedom; in a civil dispute, whether one or the other parties will lose money. I have suggested how you can become the director, author, and actor with your family while studying the Torah and capture a sense of excitement together that only reading the text may not provide.

Were I to define myself as a person, I would say that I am a Jew, deeply committed to the survival of the Jewish people within their tradition. I do not prescribe how each person should enter that tradition. I do want to help others consider the tradition.

Mary Kennan, editor, Prentice Hall Press, which is publishing this book, saw my magazine article "What's in This Week's Torah?" and invited me to develop a book on how to teach moral values using a religious text.

I agreed that a book dealing with how to discuss moral values on a regular basis could be created. My professional life has brought to my attention an unusual assortment of questions regarding ethical conduct because many persons are often placed in situations where right conduct is an issue. I have dealt with excruciating problems for clients in government, business, legal, and medical professions, in management and labor. In addition to dealing with business problems, I have prosecuted murderers and thieves and defended an assortment of persons accused of criminal activity. I have met persons who daily demonstrate exhilaration in working for the well-being of the community whereas others are callous or destructive to the community.

Our family Torah discussions at Friday night dinner, our Shabbat dinner, was intended to do three things: elevate the level of discussion, allow us to study together, and do something that was interesting for us, the parents.

I did not have the benefit of much of a Jewish education during my Texas childhood. I was immersed in an emotionally strong identification with the Jewish people and some ritual observance. I have no formal academic credentials in Judaic studies, but I have persistently studied from the time I first arrived at Harvard College and went to the Hillel House, my first exposure to Judaism on an intellectually demanding level.

Marrying at thirty-six, I have made up for lost time. Ellen, my wife, and I now have five children—first three boys, with the oldest eleven, and then two girls, five and three years of age. They know that membership in this family is an admission ticket to regular Torah conversations. The family conversations are not designed for children only. My wife, whose Jewish education was minimal as a child, welcomed this opportunity for each of us to learn.

Comments of Suzanne Stutman

From the beginning I wanted to know more. My father was a Polish immigrant who arrived in this country at age thirteen. He was unschooled in Jewish learning. Though we were not observant on a day-to-day basis, we nevertheless, as a family, my father, mother, brother, sister, and I, created and shared beautiful moments around the High Holidays. We walked to and from the synagogue on the holidays holding hands. At synagogue, I read through the High Holiday prayer book, savoring my father's pronunciation. I am sure that he prayed by rote. He had never really learned how to read Hebrew—or had long since forgotten. Although my parents were not observant, I always sensed that they were serious Jews with no doubt about their religious identification, conviction, and dedication to Jewishness. I had no idea what the Torah was beyond an assortment of disjointed stories, but miraculously I emerged from childhood with my Jewish identity firmly intact.

As was customary in my community, I attended Hebrew school and prepared for a short Bat Mitzvah on a Friday evening. My principal memory of my Bat Mitzvah centers not on the Torah portion of the week, but on the pink satin dress I wore (and still have). As if I couldn't or wouldn't escape my immigrant heritage, I never mastered Hebrew, and well into adulthood my Hebrew enunciation resembled my father's—halting and alien sounding. Even as a young woman, my Hebrew—expressed exclusively in prayer—was stimulated by and modeled after familiar sounds in the synagogue.

There was no Jewish lightning bolt that struck me, no watershed experience that moved me closer to my Jewishness. Instead, my desire for a fuller knowledge and understanding of Judaism evolved slowly, beginning while I was completing graduate school in social work at the University of Pennsylvania. At that time, I decided to keep a kosher home without fully understanding why I had made that decision or what it meant to observe the Jewish dietary laws. Several years later when my daughter, Shira, was born, I asked my father-in-law to prepare a ceremony with a Jewish ritual base so that she might be sanctified and presented to the Jewish community with the same fanfare that is accorded Jewish baby boys. A few years later, following the birth of my son, Zachary, my husband and I began to attend synagogue regularly and even tried to establish a Havurah or group of like-minded persons who were interested in seeing what Judaism might offer.

Once we moved to Washington, the pace of my evolution quickened. We joined a well-organized and highly motivated Havurah and an independent study group as well. In retrospect, my husband, Ned Stutman, served as a bridge in helping me move from a world of comparative ignorance about the value of Judaism to a place where I could learn.

This daughter of an immigrant father even sits, probably like her grandfather did, on a wooden bench on cold winter evenings listening to a wise rabbi teach Talmud, the most complex exposition of Jewish law, and has obtained a master's degree in Jewish education.

In wondering how I got to this spiritual place, I was struck by the degree to which my evolution toward Judaism and my Jewishness paralleled my professional experience as a psychotherapist. The more experience I gained as a psychotherapist, the closer I came to Judaism. At first I thought this juxtaposition ironic, since psychotherapy is a rationalistic discipline and religion, for the most part, ultrarational. How could a commitment to one inspire and coexist with a commitment to the other? The answer is simple. As I evolved in my practice, I intuited two principles that both led me (unconsciously, I'm sure) to my Jewishness and spurred me to collaborate on this book. First, I saw the extent to which people need to be able to locate their own personal spiritual refuge from the alienating and anxiety-ridden culture with which we all must contend. Second, people need a clearly defined set of truly ethical standards to use in deciding which options they will select on a day-to-day basis. For me, Judaism the religion offered the possibility for refuge, and Jewishness as reflected in the laws of the Torah offered an ethical standard of living. Collaborating on this book provides me with an opportunity to share the fruit of my experience by promoting an activity that can lead families to discover together their own spiritual refuge and ethical standards.

By design, this book emphasizes the importance of regularizing a process for families spending time together in spiritual and ethical pursuits. The importance of the process component cannot be overstated since it, like the ethics learned in it, is transferable to other contexts. As a school psychologist I have learned that families who encourage freedom in conversation on one subject generally offer it across the board. Unfortunately the converse is also true.

And so this book represents the convergence of several important loves to which I now devote much of my life—my love of Judaism, its richness and endless potential for raising expectations about the possibilities for human living; my love and respect for children, their openness and willingness to learn; my belief that children and parents have powerful lessons they can share only if they are together on a regular basis; and my love of learning for the sake of learning.

1

A REASON YOU ARE CONSIDERING TORAH TALK

URI THE SLAVE AND
YOUR FIRST TORAH DISCUSSION

Your ability to engage in conversation is the start of family Torah discussion. Imagine you are riding in an airplane. You start a conversation with the person seated next to you. "What do you do for a living?" He replies, matter of factly, "I'm a Hebrew slave." You are startled but recover smoothly by asking another question about what he does and how he got into this line of work.

Questions rush to mind as curiosity lengthens the list. Does he like it? Is it a career decision, or can he move into another form of employment?

As you consider the appropriateness of asking another question, your seatmate senses your intense curiosity. He tries to place you at ease and says, "This will help you understand me better." He hands you a slip of paper that reads:

> If you buy a Hebrew slave, he shall serve for six years, but
> in the seventh year, he is to be set free without liability.
> (Mishpatim, Exodus 21:2)*

This is a most unusual résumé. The flight is long and you are accustomed to talking with friendly strangers on tedious journeys. This man appears willing to talk about his status. Perhaps the best way to talk to him is to look at this résumé and ask the questions that come to mind, since you really have no experience in talking with a person who defines himself as a slave without using the term figuratively, as a "slave" to a job or to an unpleasant situation.

You look again at the passage, and your mind quickly sees the possibility for some interesting questions even though you know nothing about Hebrew slavery or the Torah. Now you want to know how slavery fit into life in antiquity, and how the Jewish sages dealt with an institution that seems so contrary to the idea of man in the divine image.

---

*All biblical citations are from *The Living Torah*, unless otherwise noted.

You know a little something about how to obtain information in the course of everyday life. You start at the beginning of the topic with the slip of paper with the passage to start on this part of the conversation. You ask a few questions prompted by each phrase.

"The passage says, 'If you buy a Hebrew slave'; does that mean that you were sold into slavery and someone has purchased you? Who had the authority to order your sale? Who may bid, how was your value established, and why did it happen?"

The slave, who has introduced himself as Uri, responds lightly, "You certainly have an appetite for questions, but I will talk about my predicament. A court sold me to the highest bidder when I was unable to pay a debt I owed."

"You mean you became a slave just because you owe some money? That's outrageous," you say, unable to resist giving your own views immediately. "In our society we have bankruptcy laws designed to help poor people to live with dignity when they are unable to pay their debts. Even debtors' prisons were abolished more than a century ago."

"Well, I guess I left something out. The reason I owed some money was that I was found guilty of having stolen valuable possessions worth thousands of shekels from a family in Shechem. When arrested, I had only a few shekels and several persons testified that I had squandered the money in gambling and a few other activities I'd rather not discuss now. Mind you, I'm not agreeing as to precisely what occurred, but I did not have a good defense. I was ordered either to return the possessions to the Shechem family or pay their value. Now, if I'd had some good luck in some games I play with a few fellows, I would have been able to pay. The ingrates would not lend me money to play. I couldn't put that kind of money together any other way. My relatives said that I am not upholding the family name and showed no sympathy. Actually, who wants to have anything to do with dullards like them; they sweat in the fields, planting barley and wheat, and don't ever have a good time."

The conversation continues. I ask the other questions that come to mind while looking at Uri's résumé. The passage easily suggests further questions, as do Uri's responses.

What determines the duration of a slave's term of servitude, and what work can the master require the slave to perform?

Can a slave buy himself out of the term if he legitimately obtains money, as through inheritance?

Why is the seventh year so significant in providing freedom

for the slave? Indeed, a slave may decide that he has a better arrangement with his master in terms of food and a clean, warm room and does not want to give up slavery because the work is not really so bad, and the life is better than the one he led previously.

As the plane is beginning preparations for landing, other questions come to mind about whether slavery applies to both men and women, and do any rules vary depending on gender? What about the slave's family, spouse and children, during the period of ownership, and who gets the proceeds of any work done by each of them?

Uri the Hebrew slave, the person next to you on the airplane, can answer these questions because the answers vitally concern him, affecting his life for at least six years, possibly longer. To get your sympathy, Uri refers to himself as a slave. You begin to question whether he is telling you the whole truth as he describes his life in slavery. He tells you about how the servant is forced to accept freedom when the time of service is completed, and who is to blame if he chooses to remain a slave. You begin to think that a more accurate description is that Uri is an indentured servant who has traded freedom for a specific number of years in exchange for meeting the obligation to compensate the victims of his crime—not that anyone would voluntarily want to be either, but the differences are significant.

American history provides illustration of the differences between indentured servants and slaves. Some white persons agreed to perform services for a period of years in order to pay off debts and obtain passage to the Colonies. Many early settlers of Georgia were indentured servants. Black slaves were treated quite differently, without any recognition of human rights.

This leads you to reflect, during a pause in the conversation, on what we do today. What rights to compensation does a victim of crime have? Criminal offenders generally do not pay for damage they have caused. Courts occasionally require a criminal to perform some type of service that directly reimburses the victim for injury or loss of property. The reason is not only to provide relief to the victim but also to make the criminal understand the extent of the suffering he or she has caused.

The airplane arrives at its destination. At the baggage claim, you bid farewell to Uri, with more questions creeping into your mind. During the taxi ride, you continue to think about this unusual encounter, vaguely aware that what you have learned has significance. At your hotel room, you pick up a Bible on the night table next to the telephone and search and locate the passage Uri had given you. As you flip through a few pages, the conversation with Uri keeps running through your mind. "Perhaps I'll sit down and read this book someday," you tell yourself.

You have always had an awareness of the Bible. You were never quite comfortable either in reading it or upon seeing it in your hotel room. On the few occasions when you tried to read a few passages, the writing seemed obscure, disjointed, and archaic. Having it on the hotel night table seemed like inappropriate religiosity.

Strictly speaking, what is on the hotel night table is not the Book of the Jews, though it contains the words of the Jewish version. Christian theology sees the Jewish version as the Old Testament, which was replaced by the message of the New Testament. Together they form the Christian version of the Bible. The Jewish Bible is called the Tanach in Hebrew and contains three major sections: the Torah (Five Books of Moses), the Prophets, and the Writings. Torah is the term we will use to refer to the text that is central to our concern. We will describe how family study of the Torah provides coherence to the life of a Jewish family.

A man came to Menahem Mendel of Kotzk and asked how he could make his sons devote themselves to the Torah.

Menahem Mendel answered:
"If you really want them to do this, then you yourself must spend time over the Torah, and they will do as you do. Otherwise, they will not devote themselves to the Torah but will tell their sons to do it. And so it will go on.

"If you yourself forget the Torah, your sons will also forget it, only urging their sons to know it, and they will forget the Torah and tell their sons that they should know it. And no one will ever know the Torah."

THE TRADITIONAL REASON

A man came to Menahem Mendel of Kotzk and asked how he could make his sons devote themselves to the Torah.

Who is the unnamed man who comes to Menahem Mendel of Kotzk, why does he come, and what prompts this question?

The story allows us to assume that the man is not a learned and traditional observant Jew whose regimen for life and educating his children is well defined. Such a knowledgeable person would not need to ask the question.

We assume the man is uncertain or disquieted about what his children are learning or doing. The children are missing something, and the father feels unable to provide what is missing. The man does not know enough about Torah to embrace it, nor has he fallen into the trap of rejecting it based on ignorance.

In contemporary terms, the man is a liberally educated, worldly individual. He is giving his children all that the modern world offers, but he is vaguely concerned. Something prompts a quest for tradition, the memory of an idea or the stirring of an emotion, possibly a chance reading of the insight of a sage, a random curiosity, or the example of another family.

The man summons his courage, stifles his embarrassment, and seeks out Menahem Mendel of Kotzk, a very intense, austere, early-nineteenth-century historical personality who represents a tradition with which the man has limited familiarity.

What will the man ask? How can I teach my children to be like me? Most parents do want children to accept and follow their values in some form. Apparently, the man is not certain that he alone can consciously transmit values. The man recognizes the Torah as the generator of the values to which he ascribes. He wants to increase the probabilities of his children's acceptances of these values. He feels uncertain about how to talk about values, ethics, and appropriate conduct to his children.

The question the man formulates is not "How can I make my child happier, successful, away from bad friends, drugs, idleness, and trouble?" The question is "How can I get my children to devote themselves to the Torah?"

The tradition is that God revealed the Torah at Mount Sinai. Torah is elastic as a concept. At its most taut, the Torah is the five books of Moses—Bereshith (Genesis), Shemoth (Exodus), VaYikra (Leviticus), BeMidbar (Numbers), and Devarim (Deuteronomy). At its most elastic, the Torah is the entirety of Jewish learning encompassing the vast body of literature whose very names bear the ring of ancient debates and difficult-to-penetrate learning: the Mishna, Gemara, Talmud, Tosafoth, and Shulchan Aruch.

Today's parent, for reasons that are not easily described, wants to provide his or her son or daughter with a coherent system of values, a world view, based on a millennial value system. The modern person is no longer certain that he or she can reject the ancient learning merely by dismissing it as old-fashioned or obscure. An increasing number of contemporary persons, thoroughly integrated in Western thought, music, art, and literature, recognize that the truly liberal mind must seek to understand an ancient but viable tradition without prejudice and on its own terms.

Menahem Mendel answered: "If you really want them to do this, then you yourself must spend time over the Torah, and they will do as you do."

Children place value on what adults do. The child quickly distinguishes between activities relegated only to children and those imprinted with status by adults. A typical child's attraction to sports and its heroes arises from the simple fact that adults place value on athletic skill. A child who can throw a ball through a hoop dreams of becoming a superstar as an adult, although the distance in knowledge and skill between now and then is immense.

In the matter of the moral values, the child already has the capacity to throw the ball through the hoop—the ability to know certain rights and wrongs: don't steal, don't lie. The child will not know how these moral concepts apply to countless ambiguous situations. Adults confront many quandaries in any active life in deciding what is right or wrong and how to tell the difference. If the child together with the parents confronts some of these quandaries, then all will recognize that dealing with moral issues is an adult concern in a process that requires constant learning.

A child who is involved only in children's activities learns that these are not taken seriously by adults and that in time they should be discarded. A child who participates in adult activities knows that these are regarded as long lasting.

For some societies, a child's passage into adulthood may be marked by an act of physical bravery, like going on a buffalo hunt.

"Otherwise, they will not devote themselves to the Torah but will tell their sons to do it. And so it will go on."

Some parents say, "We don't observe any rituals or engage in any religious learning. However, when our child is older, we will light the Sabbath candles and have a Passover Seder so the child will know he is a Jew."

A parent should not do anything for the sake of the children if the parent wants to influence children. An activity for the sake of the child is not one that either the parent or the child accepts as part of an adult's life. Telling a child to do something that is contrary to or inconsistent with the conduct of the parent is not an innoculation that is likely to take. If all that is being passed on is the message to do something, the content of the message is lost.

"If you yourself forget the Torah, your sons will also forget it, only urging their sons to know it, and they will forget the Torah and tell their sons that they should know it. And no one will ever know the Torah."

Nineteenth-century theorists of natural history offered the view that physical characteristics of a species could change through external physical changes. Cutting a cat's tail off would in time mean that the descendant cats would be born with bobbed tails. Experience proved that species did not evolve in this manner. A cut-off appendage in a parent animal was not missing in the offspring. By contrast, values, traditions, and language forgotten in one generation are likely to be lost forever.

Menahem Mendel tells the man precisely what will occur in two or three generations if a father tells his son of his moral commitment but does not act out the moral commitment. What is first lost is the basis for the moral commitment, the Torah. Then, in time, no one will know the Torah and conduct based on moral commitments will erode. This book tells how to teach the Torah, parent to child. The reason to do so is an individual decision. We suggest some reasons, though not precisely in language Menahem Mendel would have known.

2

YOU CAN CONDUCT FAMILY TORAH TALK

START WITH WHAT YOU KNOW

Your ability to engage in conversation is the start of family Torah discussion. Torah conversation relies on an agreed-upon topic that is different from the bulk of our social conversations and easier than informal social conversation. Planned conversation does not mean it is stilted. Conversations flow more smoothly when the conversants agree on the topic. The general topic and approach are planned, but the direction a conversation takes is far from predictable. A chance question or comment can hurdle a conversation in a new direction faster than an airplane changing course.

Build a Conversation by Instinct

A passage about slavery that appeared to have little promise for a discussion about matters of interest to you and your family has already demonstrated that a discussion can develop beyond the obvious point that slavery is bad. We began the conversation with Uri the slave on our imaginary airplane trip without knowing anything about the Torah passage. We relied on how conversations develop between strangers. We try to find out what the other person does for a living and ask questions that flow from the information given. If we ask about work and the response is "physician," the next question is often "what specialty and where." If the answers are "space medicine and living on a space station circling the moon" the questions that flow will be somewhat different than if the response is "Hansen's disease, at a lepers hospital in Africa." Each physician has a great deal to tell us. The general topics of our inquiry in each situation are likely to go to the nonscientific aspects of the work and focus on the living conditions, the nature of the general work, the problems that arise, the prospects for the future, and the dangers encountered, overcome, or still to be confronted.

Each of us knows how to participate in conversations. None of us ever formally studied a course labeled "Conversations." We have probably given little thought to the conversation process by analyzing differences among conversationalists or determining why some conversations are satisfying and others dull. We do know that some people are more interesting conversationalists than others. The difference is not necessarily because one is doing more interesting work or visiting exotic places. A person may return from a visit to China and talk obsessively about misplaced luggage while a better conversationalist will skillfully combine commonplace occurrences, news items, literary passages, and an episode in a television program to engage our attention.

Common to good conversation is an exchange of facts and opinions. Each participant has an opportunity to add a thought, a fact, or a quip. We leave a good conversation with a sense of well-being because we have added to our own understanding, learned some new information, or thought about a routine occurrence in a different way. Sometimes a conversation is satisfying just because we learn that others share our opinions. We are especially pleased when another person has given us additional justifications for our views. On occasion, we reluctantly recognize the benefits of modifying our views based upon the acquisition of new facts or arguments.

Our social conversations are often diffused. With strangers or distant acquaintances, finding a topic is sometimes a problem. We occasionally grope to find a common interest in current events, a television program, sports, or mutual acquaintances. A shared common inconvenience, such as an airport delay or stalled traffic, is a frequent stimulus to conversation even between strangers. How many conversations do you recall that were prompted by a delay in a flight's departure, loss of baggage, or stalled traffic? At times, when we talk about the weather or other topics of no particular interest our social conversations are like a muscle twitch, an automatic response to fill awkward moments of silence.

With each close friend or relative we generally have a common theme that moves from one topic to another without any apparent reason. A common theme with relatives is the welfare of immediate and extended family members. Births, deaths, health, personal activities, and ceremonial occasions are ready topics. If we meet again the next day, the conversation may focus on the same theme with emphasis on different aspects. With friends, the themes also involve families and health, as well as activities, theater, sports, religion, politics, and social events.

We engage in focused conversations with employees, employers, customers, technicians, or our children's teachers. These conversations seek to achieve a limited objective. We know generally what to discuss, the information we need, and the points to ask or make to achieve certain results.

A Setting May Establish the Topic

At a political rally, the conversation will inevitably lead to the candidate's personal qualities, the opposition's blunders, the prospects for victory. A different chain of associations will emerge in other settings. A wedding will stimulate many conversations about the respective families. Funerals will occasion comments on the long life of the deceased or the tragedy of a premature death and the hardship of the immediate survivors. Any talk about our children's education will inevitably focus on the strengths and weaknesses of teachers and the educational process.

An Agreed-Upon Topic Is an Ingredient of a Planned Conversation

A randomly selected newspaper article illustrates the technique of using a topic to stimulate a far-ranging discussion. A newspaper reported that a twelve-year-old Cambodian refugee girl, after only a few years in the United States, became a local spelling-bee champion in Tennessee. At the try for the next level championship she stumbled on the word "enchilada."

Brainstorming by free association on virtually every word of this abbreviated story can lead to a discussion of interest to parents and their children:

1. Who are the Cambodians and why have they recently come to the United States?
2. How does a refugee child become quickly integrated into this country?
3. Does this need to learn English create incentives for mastering vocabulary that are not present in a child who has spoken English since birth?
4. Is "enchilada" an English word? Was it fair to ask for a word that describes a Mexican dish, although it is available in parts of the United States? The Cambodian child said she had never eaten or heard of an enchilada. What other English words are foreign in origin and describe commonly eaten foods?

With this little story you can expand your children's knowledge about Cambodia and the boat people; the motivation and rewards for hard work; the value of striving, even though the prize is not achieved; the reasons immigrants are often strivers; America's role as a nation of nations; the benefits and detriments of immigration into the United States; the importance of the English language as a unifying force of the nation; and the countries where the issue of language is a cause for conflict— Canada, Belgium. The topic lists can go in other directions: the experiences of elders in your family as immigrants and your experiences in a foreign country in wrestling with foreign terms and using inappropriate terms. Even the same English language has developed different meanings around the world. George Bernard Shaw wryly noted that England and the United States were two countries divided by a common language.

On some of these brainstormed topics, you will have an opinion, some relevant information, and a personal experience. Obviously, the more you know about the topic, the more you can contribute.

Design a Conversation about Values

A simple story can serve to generate a range of issues about moral conduct. Consider this commonplace occurrence: A boarding passenger tells a bus driver that another person is racing down the street trying to catch this bus. The driver responds, "I can't stop now, I'll get thrown off schedule," and pulls away from the curb.

If any of us had been the breathless runner seeing the bus drive off, we would have fumed at the driver's mechanical commitment to meeting a schedule and not having an ounce of compassion. A passenger already on the bus with a tight schedule to meet a connecting bus would have been relieved. The driver did not put the convenience of one person above his obligation to passengers already on the vehicle and waiting persons at later bus stops who were relying on the schedule. From these competing feelings, we can get into the unstated facts. How far away was the runner, how far behind schedule was the bus or would it become by waiting, and how much judgment is the bus driver permitted in varying from the schedule when safety is not at stake? Some of the competing values involve the driver's decision. Is the driver making a decision for the good of the many to the detriment of the few, or is the driver acting with unnecessary rigidity in disregarding the well-being of the person running to catch the bus?

Take the same story and substitute an airline and a late passenger. What if the delay was created to accommodate a passenger who may have to wait for a once-a-day or once-a-week flight to or from a remote location? Does this change the equation as to the length of delay that is appropriate?

If you can, find anecdotes in the world around you that raise questions about values and are interesting. A more readily available source of moral predicaments, however, is the Torah. You are not required to go out and invent a story for discussion. More important, the Torah stories have been the subject of intense thought for thousands of years. Commentators in every epoch all over the world have considered their moral implications. This eases your task of finding what to discuss.

Build a Conversation on a Parent's Occupation

Once you start using the Torah stories for discussion, each parent can use personal experiences as an initial method for developing an approach to discussion. An artist can discuss crafts in this context by reviewing the detailed instructions for the construction and decoration of the Tabernacle (Terumah, Exodus 26:1–36) and the Ark of the Covenant (Terumah, Exodus 25:10–22). Business people will find many Torah references to ancient management, personnel, credit, and pricing practices. Psychologists, social workers, and social scientists will find endless opportunities to apply their theories and explore the feelings or thoughts of the people whose activities the Torah reports. Lawyers can apply their knowledge and make observations about the considerable advocacy skills demonstrated by Abraham in pleading for the residents of Sodom when God threatened to destroy the city because of the wicked behavior of its residents (VaYera, Genesis 18:23–33), or by Moses in his frequent negotiations with God over whether and to what extent God should punish the Jews in the desert for their ungrateful acts (for example, Ki Thisa, Exodus 32:11–14).

The possibilities are without limit. Political scientists may find the Torah's description of the tribal organization of the children of Israel a basis for introducing some theories of this field. Whatever the topic, the Torah has a text to support discussions on agriculture, political organizations, war, diplomacy, conservation, economic development, migration, and domestic relations, among many others. Parents need not be shy about demonstrating that they "know a thing or two" about important matters.

A dividend of this approach is that family members will get to know each other better. In the days when extended families lived together "over the store," children were intimately familiar with what parents did for a living. Now, work and family are separate. Most children have little knowledge about their parents' work. Regular Torah table talk permits and encourages parents to introduce their work experience through the text. The introduction of the parent's work experience is not for the purpose of swaying the child into or away from the parent's line of work. The purpose is to make the child aware of some of the complexities in the world, as experienced by the parent, and to permit the child to understand more about what forms the parent's perspective. In turn, this may help develop within the child a greater willingness to look more closely at a wider range of persons and activities.

Invite Commentators to Help Build the Conversation

We cannot always arrange to have fascinating guests as our conversation partners. If you could, then you might have a warm, witty, and engaging individual to encourage the children's interests. Of course, a parent is that engaging individual on some topics. To give texture to the conversation, we have found that families must use the insights of the commentaries on the Torah, the written observations of individuals who have over the thousands of years studied the Torah. The sages have brainstormed the Torah and are able to generate ideas, give information, and take you down unexpected conversational paths. The sages are always available to be guests without your having to set the table for extra persons. Commentaries come in all sizes, approaches, and degrees of simplicity or complexity, as does the grouping within which you will conduct the family conversation about Torah.

PRODUCING THE BEST
FAMILY TALK SHOW IN TOWN

The Cast

The production of a family talk show requires adherence to the following principles:

1. A parent who is prepared and will conduct the discussion.

2. Regular weekly discussions, preferably at Friday evening Shabbat dinner.
3. Insistence that children attend.

A Group Must Have a Leader

At least one parent must accept the responsibility of preparing and leading the Torah conversation. The decision as to which parent leads may emerge based on father/mother roles or the personalities and interests of the parents. For the father, leading the conversation may be one of his few opportunities during the week where he is unhurriedly with the family. He has this occasion to place his imprint on the life of the family. The mother who is employed outside the home may also seize this opportunity to nurture her relationship with the family by leading the Torah conversation. The parents may agree that one will have primary responsibility, or they may choose to rotate leadership on a fixed schedule.

The subject matter may determine who will lead the conversation. Any basis is acceptable as long as the matter is resolved well in advance of the discussion. If the parents wait to negotiate responsibility at the dinner table, then the children will conclude that the discussion is not viewed seriously.

A Group Must Have a Fixed Time for Meeting

We favor having a regular discussion coupled with a weekly Friday evening meal. This Shabbat meal has anchored Jewish life in the family. The regularity of weekly Shabbat eve creates a powerful force for Torah discussion. The time allotted for the meal will include time for the discussion. The regularity will also facilitate preparation for the discussion. Continuity will exist. Topics discussed the previous week but left unfinished can be picked up or can serve as the basis for further discussion. Of course, Torah discussion can be conducted on other occasions with the same family group. Most important is the establishment of a firm time and place that takes priority over any other predictable demand for time.

Members of the Group Must Attend Meetings

Every member of the family is expected to attend, we hope to participate, and at the least, not to obstruct. Introducing a new type of family activity where no such practice exists may be met with different degrees of enthusiasm or opposition by teenagers. Teenagers may overcome their initial reluctance to attend when they find the discussions are a good opportunity to let a parent know what they are thinking. The teenager may use the Torah characters and predicaments to indirectly make points that are of present and personal concern.

In family Torah discussion we do not get to select our partners. The number of persons in your family and the ages of the children are givens. When spoons hit the table and gravy spills to the floor, when the children do not appear to pay the slightest attention, you will wonder why you were not able to attract a better quality of conversation partners.

However, children of three years of age are ready and will participate enthusiastically. Even younger ones will occasionally join. Torah conversation is easiest to start when the children are young, if my own experience is any guide.

"What's in this week's Torah?" my young son once asked when we sat down to our Shabbat eve meal. This question starts a lively discussion. We turn to the page in the Torah portion where we stopped the previous week and discover that Lot has left his uncle, Abraham, and gone with his family and flock to the best pastures near the city of Sodom. (Lekh Lekha, Genesis 13:8 – 13) God has doomed Sodom to destruction. My eight-year-old, Jeremy, asks why. I tell about the wickedness of Sodom's inhabitants, then explain how Abraham bargains with God to save Sodom. The family's excitement increases. We take roles. Jeremy pretends he is Lot fleeing from the city. Six-year-old Asher is Lot's wife. I instruct him not to look back at the destruction of Sodom or "be consumed." I test Asher's curiosity by pointing animatedly behind his back to nonexistent goings-on. He turns around, just as did Lot's wife, whose backward glance resulted in her becoming a pillar of salt. My third son, Barak, is four. He knows the names of the characters and asks sensible questions. I ask my two-year-old daughter, Dina, a multiple-choice question: Was Abraham's wife called Connie, Linda, or Sarah?

We try to understand why Sodom was destroyed. I tell them the surprising answer of the rabbis. The city of Sodom with all its inhabitants was destroyed because of its people's unremitting hostility to strangers. We then take a closer look at the story, see that the rabbis have a basis for reaching this moral, and conclude the discussion either by summarizing what we have learned or just letting the point remain on the table for each to digest according to the child's understanding.

The children are now three years older since that discussion, and a fifth child, Kira, has come into the family. When she was two and one half, she already insisted on receiving a role assignment. The interest of the other children in the weekly discussion remains enthusiastic.

Spilled wine or a shrill whine is the common denominator for all families with young children at a Shabbat dinner. A multitude of other no more serious human-made calamities occur during family Torah conversation, predictably at the most dramatic point. Forge ahead. Do not permit the discussion to lag even while catching freshly spilled Concord grape wine before it drips to the rug. The perfect discussion leader will keep the participants interested and the discussion going despite distractions and occasional boredom. This requires knowledge, communications skill, and creativity. These three elements can create an atmosphere for learning that is within the grasp of each of us.

Parents know certain teaching techniques. They learn what works and what does not. Nonetheless, steps and skills unique to conducting a conversation about Torah need highlighting.

1. Pledging the family oath
2. Managing the family
3. E Pluribus Unum—out of many, one
4. Setting the good example
5. Lending the unobtrusive helping hand

1. Pledging the Family Oath

The producer of the good family talk show makes a commitment to have the show each and every week at a specified time. We have suggested Friday night, but the principle is the same if you choose another day or hour. A parent will have to avoid any other commitments for that time if the children are to believe that the parent is serious about the benefits of Torah discussion. An "on-again, off-again" process will not work.

Children may balk initially and struggle against this new requirement, not because they have any well-founded reason but just because they view this activity as a new form of discipline. Parents can deal with this reluctance by emphasizing the importance of the occasion and the obligation to attend. The parent should give the reasons this type of family discussion is so highly regarded and that only exceptional circumstances can interfere with this rhythm of family life. The positive interest in the discussion itself will eventually replace the child's initial objections. Also, each of the family members will develop a commitment to the group. This can become the individual's pledge to the group, the tie that binds a soldier to his buddies, the athlete to his teammates. Any small group that engages in regularized activity and depends on the attendance of each for its survival depends on individual loyalty.

2. Managing the Family

Authoritative parents produce children with vitality, optimism, and competence. An authoritative parent is firm, gives reasons for specific conduct, and accepts modifications that do not hinder reaching the central goal. By contrast, an authoritarian parent lays down the law, plain and simple. Another contrast is the parent who has no firm convictions and will permit the children to make all the choices affecting family life. Parents have usually developed through a series of random unrelated experiences a certain style of being "in charge," or managing others. This personal management style may have little coherence or internal consistency.

People who manage other people for a living receive special training in management techniques. They must manage employees while maintaining a suitable level of morale. The principles of good management include planning the discussion, developing reasonable goals for each child, and communicating those expectations at the outset. To implement good management, you must unambiguously set boundaries for permissible behavior, identify a goal for the group, and keep the activity moving toward achieving the goal.

In practice, you will plan a ten- to fifteen-minute conversation. Choose a topic that is of a digestible length and encompasses only a few basic points. Keep the discussion directed toward these points. End the discussion even if your children want more until, in time, you are certain that a longer discussion will not lessen enthusiasm.

Involve your children in the discussion by asking questions. Better a mediocre answer to questions than for the parent to conduct a monologue. Use the Socractic method by posing "what if" questions to challenge the reason given for reaching a particular conclusion.

We discussed earlier the moral issues that could arise from the simple circumstances of a bus driver falling behind schedule while waiting for a tardy person who is running to catch the bus as it is pulling away. Using that simple story, assume that one of the children at your table discussion concludes that the bus driver must rigidly adhere to the schedule and may never wait beyond the scheduled time for a tardy person. If so, then ask questions that explore this response.

1. What if there is only one bus a day that is driving through an isolated community and there is no other means of transportation readily available?
2. What if the tardy person is known to the bus driver to have been delayed because of some very meritorious reason, such as giving comfort to an injured person?
3. What if the delay will not adversely affect any passengers or the driver?

On the other hand, if the child says that the bus driver should wait for the tardy person, the "what if" questions might include:

1. What if the delay by the driver will cause all of the other passengers to miss a connection with an airplane flight?
2. What if the delay may bring disciplinary action upon the bus driver for failing to adhere to regulations?
3. What if the tardy person is known to the bus driver to have been delayed because of some frivolous activity?

Leave enough room for each child to speak, answer questions, and express a point of view. Encourage practice in this skill. If there is a child who needs more time to figure out an answer, all present should wait patiently. On the other hand, help your children stay close to the subject at hand, or if they wander, bring them back to the point.

Encourage and plan participatory activities to express the central idea of the story in an adventuresome manner.

3. E Pluribus Unum—Out of Many, One

The leader will have to concentrate on including everyone in the discussion. The leader must find the way to encourage each individual into participation. For some, a good story will suffice. Others will require questions directed to their age and intelligence, and still others will remain aloof until a game is suggested with a juicy role to play. An atmosphere of involvement is infectious. A wave of involvement will push even a shy child into the group's common endeavor.

A child's failure to respond may have little to do with the discussion and may not even be a lack of interest or poor manners. The exciting challenge for the leader is to bring each non-participant into the discussion. Making a challenge of a trying situation will positively affect the outcome. One political figure observed that shaking hands with thousands of prospective voters was not the boring and demanding trial one might imagine. He conceived of the handshake as a twenty-second opportunity to make a lifetime impression on an individual who, in turn, would pass that impression on to others. Put this way, each handshake was a challenge to be taken and conquered.

Similarly, the leader who responds to the challenge of the recalcitrant child by showing that each person's ideas are valued is more likely to succeed. This is illustrated by an incident involving a young girl's halting reading of the text that touched off her negative reaction. Having concluded the few sentences, she slouched in her chair, and her body language conveyed her boredom and disinterest. Obviously, she was embarrassed by her poor reading and decided to "drop out" rather than risk another invitation to read. The leader sought to recapture the girl's interest by asking a question addressed specifically to her: whether the commandment "honor thy father and thy mother" means that children must obey unfair or unreasonable requests from their parents even when they acquire maturity as teenagers. Her eyes looked up, she turned toward the table, and, reconnecting with the discussion, began making a real contribution. She was talking about a subject in which she was an expert—the relationship between a parent and a teenager.

4. Setting the Good Example

Adults in general, and parents in particular, give significant behavioral cues for children. Words do not communicate a person's attitudes; behavior does. A parent's attitude on family conversation about the Torah is quickly imitated by younger children.

A child watching a parent prepare for Torah table talk learns that the activity is regarded as important. This recognition is more lasting than a hundred pronouncements on the importance of Torah table talk.

The way the discussion itself is conducted has impact. If everyone is free to interrupt another before the thought is finished, then the discussion is soon dominated by the most forceful personalities, and the more reticent individuals will withdraw.

5. Lending the Unobtrusive Helping Hand

Torah table talk participants should always remember that both the people and the vehicle of ideas are important in this activity, but giving more value to ideas at the expense of people lessens the joy and purpose of Torah table talk.

People learn best when their efforts are positively rewarded. Unfortunately, this rule bears repeating since it can be honored more in the "breach" than in the doing. Sometimes we unconsciously show off how much we know, just like muscle men on the beach show off by flexing their muscles. In any event, it is not always easy to appreciate the value of someone else's comment if we can't immediately see how it bears directly on a point under discussion. If a comment goes over like a lead balloon and is ignored, the commentator will quickly and quietly retreat, probably never to be heard from again. Even worse, a retreat can turn into a rout if the comment is criticized, even by a seemingly innocuous response like, "I don't see it that way."

Children are vulnerable to negative criticism because they are often unsure of themselves. A lack of confidence or fear may appear as silliness when a child tries to participate. Fortunately, a child can have a personal feeling of well-being without too much effort on the part of the parents. A child's comments deserve full attention and need and deserve a substantive response. Sometimes, all a child needs is recognition for taking the risk of making a comment. A discussion on the reason for God's command to Moses not to enter the Promised Land (Pinchas, Numbers 27:12–14) provoked a question from my five year old, Zachary. He piped up, "Was Moses punished for being afraid?" A short exchange followed about whether his parent would ever punish him for being afraid. Quite correctly, Zachary was assured that he would not be punished for having fears, no matter how unfounded. He was then praised for asking a thought-provoking question. The Torah passage was cited as evidence that Moses was not punished for having fears but for specific misconduct. My son left the table conversation satisfied with his participation. He had also received a comforting response that he would not ever be penalized merely because he expressed fear.

Often, if a child is drawn out, a link exists between a child's comment and the discussion, even where the comment appears inappropriate. The responses of a child or adult originate from within the personal experience range. To understand the response fully requires finding the linkage to the person's experience.

The observations of the older children should be valued whether or not it is the conclusion offered by those who have delved into the question more deeply. Not every answer is correct, of course, but disagreement is positive if the discussion leaves everyone thinking about all the conflicting views and their respective justifications.

The discussion concerning God's prohibition on Moses against entering the Promised Land, which was treated one way with the young child, might go in a different direction with an older child who makes several arguments that the punishment that prohibited Moses from going into the Promised Land was too severe. Moses had an outstanding career in leading the Israelites out of Egypt and in guiding them through forty difficult years in the desert. All Moses did was strike the rock to bring forth water when he was instructed merely to speak to the rock and water would gush forward. (Chukath, Numbers 20:7–13) At most, his lapse in obedience to God's command did not warrant taking away a final fulfillment.

Others acknowledged that even though Moses' punishment was severe it was appropriate precisely because he was such an outstanding personality. They echoed the view of some rabbinic authorities that the greater the person, the higher the expectations. A small infringement for an average person is considered as a very serious failing in a great person with the consequences appropriate to the character and status of the person. This remains true, for we continue to judge the conduct of our leading political, religious, and moral authorities by a higher standard than we do for others. This argument gives everyone at the table an entirely different way of judging a person's conduct.

THE SCRIPT

On the Level Plane

The Torah portion is almost always sufficiently rich in story and meaning to permit a discussion geared to the understanding of any age level.

The level or levels at which a discussion is conducted depends in large part on the ages of the participants. A rough division of age groups suggests three groupings.

Level 1. With very young children present (ages three to seven) the leader must rely on simplified facts and exciting activities. Verbal analysis by such young children is best achieved by presenting them with multiple choice questions.

Example. Was Abraham migrating to: (a) New Jersey; (b) California; (c) Caanan?

The value and use of art and drama as expressive forms cannot be overstated. With this age group in particular, you must act out the story even while directing from the dinner table. When excessive energy is present, the child and parents can build other props with paint and clay in preparation for the discussion. (See in Chapter 4: "Hands On: Constructions Large and Small.")

Level 2. With children between ages eight and twelve, the reliance on artistic or dramatic expressive forms can diminish in favor of expressing creative thought. Game playing is especially suitable for this group. Organizing the questions so as to present them as a television newscast or panel show, for example, will loosen inhibitions. (See in Chapter 4: "Lights, Camera, Action.")

Level 3. With children aged twelve and up, you can have the same type of discussion that you would have with adults. You can discuss the characters, action, and plot and the moral issues that emerge. For those with a literary bent, you can engage in textual analysis. The commentaries are filled with possibilities for all or any of these approaches. Indeed, in time you may find that your older child will accept the responsibility for preparing and leading the discussion at this level. (See Chapter 5, "The Commentators.")

THREE SPRINGBOARDS INTO THE TORAH

Diving into the Torah with any age level group may cause some anxiety. What follows are some survival pointers on how to explore the environment of the Torah. The typical method of learning what is between the covers of a book is to read it from beginning to end. The English descriptive term "Bible" means a compendium of books. Paradoxically, the Torah is not well understood by reading the text straight through. We recommend against merely reading the text to the family. Reading a complex narrative with strange names and genealogical histories will undermine the rhythm of family Torah talk. Many people have probably been deterred from studying Torah after briefly scanning a few pages privately or at a synagogue. A straight reading of the text will doom the Torah conversation. Approaching the text bit by bit, for the purpose of discussion rather than recitation, will successfully launch the Torah conversation. Two or three different approaches to the topics are possible:

1. Line by line
2. The weekly portion
3. Themes

1. Line by Line

You can begin at the beginning, the Creation story. The story has immediate dramatic elements. It also raises very fundamental questions about the nature of God, the ordering of the Universe, and the role of each individual who is created in God's image. Or you may wish to start with a story that is less demanding. The story of the first Jew, Abraham (originally known as Abram), is a good beginning story. Either of the following passages can be the subject for an evening's discussion.

> God said to Abram, "Go away from your land, from your
> birthplace, and from your father's house, to the land that I
> will show you." (Lekh Lekha, Genesis 12:1)

The discussion could focus on the disruption and upheaval experienced by Abraham in response to God's command, the order of references to land, birthplace, and father's house. You could introduce the hardships of the immigrant experience within your family's history, comparing the differences and similarities with the circumstances experienced by Abraham. An obvious distinguishing characteristic is that Abraham's decision was based on faith, which permits an excursion into how a man of faith is depicted in the Torah.

The next week you could focus primary attention on the lines of the Torah that follow. With the line-by-line approach, you need only to briefly recall the characters, the setting, and the previous week's discussion. You will find that the following lines will present new ideas for discussion and are not merely elaborations on the preceding lines.

> I will make you into a great nation. I will bless you and
> make you great. You shall become a blessing. I will bless
> those who bless you, and he who curses you, I will
> curse. All the families of the earth will be blessed through
> you. (Lekh Lekha, Genesis 12:2–3)

Older children could take the affirmative and negative of the proposition of whether God's promise to Abraham was fulfilled through the course of Jewish history. This could lead into a discussion of why the Jews have flourished despite circumstances that should rationally have caused the Jews to wither. On the other hand, if one takes the "vale-of-tears" approach to Jewish history, then the fruits of the blessing may at times not appear all that obvious.

With the line-by-line approach, the family is not concerned about how far the discussion goes at any particular time. Preparation is made easier because what you have read in the commentaries on a topic will serve for these later discussions. The amount of the discussion is always within manageable limits. The only goal is to hold a good conversation on the Torah, not to cover a given amount of material.

Above all, do not become impatient. The line-by-line approach is like the drip irrigation method pioneered in Israel, where small measured quantities of water are piped directly to plants cultivated in arid zones. Scientists have learned that many plants will flourish without being showered or sprayed by water. Drip irrigation is direct, regular, and controlled, and conserves water while providing only as much as the plant can absorb. The cumulative impact is seen in the sturdy growth of a well-watered plant. Our family took three years of weekly conversations to complete the chapters of Bereshith (Genesis). The process is important, not the finish line.

2. The Weekly Portion

Planning the discussions on the weekly Torah portion will impose the discipline of the calendar on your Torah table talk. Your topic is preselected. Also, the value of the discussion is reinforced when at the Shabbat services the same portion is read, and the rabbi's sermon or the comments of a Bar or Bat Mitzvah is based on its content. You will have a head start, having already noted a significant meaning within the text or learned the answer to a point that is raised at the service. The Torah is divided into portions, parshioth, with the same weekly portion read in every synagogue in the world. The portion read on a given Shabbat is called the parshah, and is the portion of the week. The cycle commences each year on the first Shabbat after the holiday of Simchat Torah, when the first portion of Bereshith (Genesis) is read. Then, week after week, the succeeding portions are read until the entire Torah is completed on the following Simchat Torah. The cycle has been repeated each year for thousands of years. The very fact of adhering to the cycle of reading the Torah places the discussion in a powerful rhythm.

A Torah story has impact far beyond the moral values inherent in it. When you discuss this story, you are also connected with others in your community and throughout the world who are discussing this text and these commentaries. You and your family are establishing a tie with history and with a wider community at the same time—a rather remarkable achievement to arise from a conversation about one story per week.

Over time the impact of the discussions is to create a common language for your child and yourself with others who learn from the Torah. Texture is added to the personality of each family member, and a common culture develops for sharing with others. Adding a culture to one's knowledge is as enriching as learning a new language. Properly learned, a language is not just verbs and nouns but is the acquisition of a literature, culture, and history. A shared culture permits an immediate basis for establishing rapport with others by knowing another's point of view without having to go through preliminaries for developing a basis for a continuing dialogue.

For the nineteenth-century educated Englishman, the common culture included substantial knowledge of Greek and Latin classics. This permitted a richness in allusions, analogies, and metaphors. So, too, Shakespeare and the Bible were within the basic learning of educated people in America not too long ago. Today there is no general agreement as to what is required by way of common culture for an educated person. However, knowing the Torah places an individual in communication with a group through a common culture.

Skim the Torah portion narrative. You will quickly discover that each weekly portion contains many topics for discussion.

The challenge is to select one episode or idea for discussion. The early Torah text follows the unfolding of the lives of the patriarchs. The many substories add to the development of their characters and their relationships with others and God. Jumping from week to week may be disorienting until you have a general appreciation of what has principally occurred. You can successfully use this procedure if the portion selected for discussion each week is fairly short. An example follows.

Jacob flees his homeland and arrives in Haran, where his Uncle Laban resides along with Laban's two daughters, Leah and Rachel. Your Torah conversation can focus on any of a number of incidents in this immigrant's experience.

A prime incident for discussion is Laban's deception of Jacob. First, Laban agreed to present his daughter Rachel in marriage to Jacob, who loved her. In exchange, Jacob agreed to work for seven years as Laban's shepherd. Laban deviously broke his commitment by presenting his heavily veiled older daughter, Leah, at the wedding ceremony intended for Jacob and Rachel. Your family's acting group can re-create the steps leading up to Jacob's surprise and anger when he discovers the deception the morning after. (VaYetze, Genesis 28:10–32:3) Examine what alternatives Jacob, as the penniless outsider, had against Laban, the man of property and influence, who was the cause of the deceit.

3. Thematic Approach

The most ambitious effort is to use the Torah to illustrate and develop a discussion about a common theme. Normally this is easier when all the participants are familiar with the text.

Sibling relationships. Conflicts between siblings are among those most powerfully illustrated in the Torah. Frequently, the Torah describes brotherly relations that are anything but loving. You might question what the common elements are for the animosity among the following: Cain and Abel (Bereshith, Genesis 4:1–16); Ishmael and his half-brother Isaac (VaYera, Genesis 21:1–21); Esau and Jacob (Toledoth, Genesis 25:19–33, 26:34–28:9; VaYishlach, Genesis 32:4–33:17); the sons of Jacob and their brother Joseph (VaYeshev, Genesis 37).

Marital relationships. Abraham and Sarah, Isaac and Rebecca, and Jacob and his two wives, Leah and Rachel, provide much material for exploration of the marital relationships. While po-

lygamy is not a contemporary practice, the tangle of human relationships that is described in the Torah remains a human
concern.

Parents and child. The examples of these relationships range
from the extraordinary to the quite ordinary. At the one end, God
commands Abraham to take Isaac, the son he loves, and offer him
as a sacrifice. Ever the man of faith, Abraham complies without
question. Isaac is arguably aware of what is intended but does not
protest. These are, of course, extraordinary circumstances.
(VaYera, Genesis 22:1–19)

More conventionally, what parent has not experienced repeated accusations of favoring one child over the others? In developing this theme, you may wish to consider whether children
are always treated differently depending upon the order of their
birth or whether their mother was a wife or concubine of the patriarchal figure. Our contemporary experience of marriage and
remarriage has created blended families with full-, half-, and step-
brother and -sister relationships. These are formed when a husband and wife with children divorce, each remarries another
spouse who also has children, and in turn the new marriages are
fruitful. These complicated parent–child relationships bear similarities to those of antiquity.

If you want to examine the ever fascinating issue about the
development of children with powerful parents then the Torah
has some striking examples. Isaac is depicted as an essentially
passive personality, contrasting with the forceful qualities of his
father Abraham. Nonetheless, the commentators do ascribe a role
of importance for him in the patriarchal line.

By contrast, Moses has two sons, Gershom and Eliezer, who
are mentioned in passing but play no role in the unfolding drama
of the Israelite exodus from Egypt and wanderings in the desert.

The Torah's lessons are moral ones, laden with values and
models of behavior. Even a negative model has the capacity to
teach, while a positive model shows that exemplary personalities may have failings. The following example of Lot's daughters
makes this dramatic point.

Lot and his daughters seek refuge in a cave following the destruction of Sodom and the death of Lot's wife. The daughters
believe that except for their father there is no other man left in
the world to marry them in a normal manner. Believing themselves to have witnessed the end of the world, they intoxicate
their father and then, in turn, cause him to impregnate each of

them. In this disturbing manner, with the children taking the lead, are born Moab and Ammon, ancestors of the non-Jewish tribes who bore those names. (VaYera, Genesis 19:30–38)

CANCELING RESERVATIONS

Few of us have ever witnessed a family with young children gathering around the Shabbat evening dinner table in perfect tranquillity. If such there be, we imagine that a quiet word from their parents is sufficient to signal dinnertime. Each child pleasantly sets aside the task of the moment and eagerly accepts the invitation. Everyone is patiently seated at the table, shining faces awaiting eagerly the ritual, meal, and conversation.

At first glance, your family may not seem like the ideal group to discuss much of anything, to say nothing of serious topics. You may think that you need a better behaved, more serious group with more adept leaders. You are correct in voicing this as your first reservation about engaging in family Torah discussion. We will add to the list of reasons "why not" to start Torah discussion. With experience, you can make the list even longer. From our participation in family Torah discussions and that of others we will raise reservations you may not have imagined.

Responses exist for some of the reservations, while other problems are inherent in the process and will not disappear. For a few of the doubts, we will say merely that the concern is less than meets the eye.

In most families, the family dinner scene unfolds with dramatic tension. The call to come to the table is first announced. No one answers. The invitation is repeated in a more forceful voice. A faint stirring. A command is issued. A child or two begins to straggle in; one provokes the other. Other children begin to move, but not necessarily in the direction of the dining room. One child suddenly recalls the necessity to do something else or to make a quick phone call to a friend. Finally, all are gathered.

The allocation of tasks for ritual observances on Shabbat eve is an inevitable point of conflict. Even where the assignments are well known, a dispute may flare over who strikes the match to light the Shabbat candles or who pulls the cover off the challah. A child fidgets; another makes an unnecessary observation. Eventually the mood becomes more subdued and the side comments more restrained when a few prayers are recited and blessings are made. As the meal is served and eaten, the noise level inches upward.

The beginning of the family Torah discussion will focus the attention of the group despite the inevitable distractions. One child's attention will wander, another will decide to leave the table and in the process trip over a brother who will retaliate with a kick. The child who walks away from the table to get a drink in the kitchen or go to the bathroom will probably soon return, if the discussion is the main event in the household. The parents should not expect the riveted attention of the children. These irritants sometimes seem overwhelming to the parents. To the untrained eye the scene appears chaotic.

The trained eye looking at this family scene sees the underlying order: Individuals of different ages and interests have all gathered at a regular time. They are willing to discuss an agreed-upon subject matter, which may affect subsequent conduct. Weekly meetings of senior company executives bear striking similarities to your family Torah discussion: regularity, the accommodation of conflicting interests while pursuing common objectives, and the need to set policy for future action.

Occasional disruptive behavior does not necessarily mean the absence of an underlying order. Business meetings are not always conducted in carpeted rooms with paneled walls and large conference tables where no voice rises above a conversational tone. Tempers will flare if the judgment of an executive is challenged or disgruntled investors seek to make changes. Imagine a partnership breaking up, a union negotiating with management, or a group of academics voting to give tenure to a colleague. The business meeting is not always quieter than the dinner table meeting. Indeed, the most obvious difference between the two is that some of the members around the family table are not able to touch the floor with their feet.

Irritants are a natural part of most meetings. The business setting may involve annoying personalities, self-promoters, pessimists, false enthusiasts, grand promisers, and people who deal exclusively in the irrelevant. The presence of the irritants does not prevent the business meeting from going forward. We learn to accommodate each personality type so that the purpose of the meeting may be accomplished. Family irritants are no more daunting and should not be given too great a prominence. These irritants should not deter a family from having regular Torah discussions. Indeed, learning to deal with different personalities and occasionally difficult situations may teach lasting lessons.

Establishing and maintaining a commitment to meet on a regular weekly basis for Torah discussions can also become an irritant, albeit different from the distractions at the dinner table. A family that has not regularly maintained observance of the Shabbat eve will encounter problems in shifting toward regular Shabbat Torah discussion. The parents will face the adjustment of forgoing social invitations for Friday evening. The advice to start the discussions when the children are young is based on the objective fact that young children do not have many social demands, and all of them are within the control of the parents. Also, younger children thrive on the attention that this type of family gathering generates. They enjoy the social activities provided by the involvement of the parents.

Children, as they grow older, may insist that being with peers is more important than staying with the family. For families where the institution of the Shabbat-eve discussion is well established the children will usually continue the commitment to the family. Making the Shabbat table discussion a social occasion for inviting other families or your teenage children's friends may itself become an alternative social activity that diminishes the child's insistence on being with another group at that time.

The single most important ingredient in the success of establishing Torah discussion as a family institution on Shabbat Eve is the decision of the parents to do so and their consistent adherence to that decision. Four, five, or six consecutive Shabbat-eve Torah discussions will show that the parents are serious. The families that have embarked on this form of family activity are showing that a traditional background is not essential for family involvement in moral discussions.

A parent has to decide that the discussion process has value in order to have family Torah conversations. In short, Torah discussion becomes a priority along with other family commitments. If finding time for family Torah discussion is difficult, we suggest displacing one of the less important activities within the family, so that Torah discussion has a fair chance to succeed. A shifting of social commitments from Friday evening to other nights can establish a new pattern of behavior that is not only acceptable, but that, in time, may seem like the normal order of things.

Making the commitment to set aside one evening for discussion with your family on a once-a-week basis will, for some, be among the most difficult of decisions to implement. The regularity of business and social patterns is deeply ingrained for adults and older children.

You might consider what causes a person to change a pattern of behavior. Usually, it is the prospect of a golden opportunity or the need to avoid injury. A family will move across the country if a job opportunity is sufficiently attractive. A family will move away from a neighborhood if personal safety is at stake. These are the extremes.

Changes in schedule are made with less demand. Consider how you would react to a note from the teacher saying that your nursery-school child is having language development problems. A speech therapist who confirms the observations may recommend a course of twice-weekly therapy. The therapist may also express the view that it is possible that the problem will cure itself with time. However, the speech therapist adds, the problem may not cure itself and may leave long-term speech and psychological impairment. The most difficult change to make is when you are uncertain about the need for change because you may not have convincing proof that the proposed course of action will lead to the promised result or that change is needed. Nonetheless, the parent has to make the choice and do what is needed.

To overcome the reluctance to change an existing schedule of activities requires harnessing the same motivation that would have been necessary for treating the child's speech problems. The motivation for Torah talk may arise from the traditional reason why—that you want to have Jewish grandchildren by passing the tradition on through your child. Alternatively, your decision may be based on the psychological reasons offered, that the family discussion process about values leads to a healthier family. The decision may be a combination of these and other reasons. Establishing a regular program of family conversations about the Torah changes the status quo. Like every change, you may have some unexpected benefits from the activity.

For some, the decision to engage in family Torah discussion may be grounded in a parent's decision to learn more about Judaism. In this event, the family is offering the support system to the parent who needs some slight additional motivation to do the learning.

Preparation for Torah study requires the commitment of a parent's most diminished resources—time and energy. The weekly preparation time is initially viewed as a major disincentive. However, the regularity of the preparation often makes the task easier rather than more difficult. Like any other skill, once you acquire a minimum familiarity in approaching the task, the next time around is easier. Eventually, preparation for the discussion becomes a normal part of weekly life.

So, how do you find an hour a week when you already feel that every moment is committed? Some very busy people prepare for the Torah discussion while riding on trains, planes, or subways. Others fit in ten- or fifteen-minute segments of time a few times during a weekend. A quiet midweek evening can serve the same purpose. The common ingredient is a conscious decision to engage in an act of creation, setting aside a total of fifty minutes to prepare for a ten-minute conversation with your family.

If by now you have made the decision to set aside the time for preparation and for the family discussion, a special problem may arise if you feel that your Jewish experience as a child was emotionally and intellectually barren. Your feeling about Jewish traditions may resemble the parched and empty feeling of one who has crossed a wasteland like the Sinai Desert. The solitary desert traveler who straggles into town with parched lips, swollen legs, and in a state of delirium has obviously lacked the sustenance of life-giving water and the nourishment of food. The traveler has also undoubtedly suffered extremes of temperature, the absence of companionship, and the weariness of staring at a featureless landscape for too long a period.

Similarly, an adult Jew may transit childhood without any Jewish intellectual or spiritual content. The negative memories may be the result of minimal learning and empty routines. For many people knowledge about Judaism was arrested at the preteen level. In no other area of our knowledge are we content to make decisions or have careers based solely on what we learned prior to the age of thirteen. How many physicians ended their study of chemistry in the ninth grade? Now, as parents, we are faced with the prospect of educating our children about Torah based on this limited background.

How, then, you ask, can a person who has a minimal understanding of Jewish texts and is without knowledge of the Hebrew language suddenly become a teacher of those texts? The concern is legitimate. The parents who do not "know enough" to conduct a Torah discussion will find comfort in contemplating the Chinese proverb, used by President John F. Kennedy, "A journey of a thousand miles must start with the first step." Learning of any kind is always accomplished one lesson at a time. A person who begins running for exercise does not expect to compete in a marathon by the end of the first week. Even the perpetual student of the Torah never reaches a level of knowing or understanding it all, because the key to studying it is that it is a continuing process of discovering nuances and interpretations, not the mastery of a fixed body of material.

Now that you may guardedly be willing to try and teach your children some Torah at the family table, you have another worry. What is the impact of the discussion likely to be on my children? Will it make them too observant or will the regimen drive them entirely away from any connection with Judaism? Will the conversation get too personal?

Family Torah discussion alone is unlikely to lead a child to adopt the garb and practices of the most intensely observant Jews. On the other hand, no one can prove that failure to teach your child Jewish values and practices will inevitably lead to membership in an Eastern cult. In short, starting down the path of Torah discussion is no more than a thoughtful step. Wherever it leads, it gives a healthy structure and content to the family at this time. Generally, the best insurance that the child grows up, more or less, with the value system you seek to impart is to make the discussion about values an integral part of the family experience, which is precisely what Torah discussion does.

Torah discussion permits a family the option of conversations on personal matters. Families are normally accustomed to conversations on functional or factual matters about "How did you do in school?" or "Who won the baseball game?" A family may feel unprepared for conversations about values that lead to discussions about personal attitudes, beliefs, or feelings. A Torah story can naturally lead into a family discussion on a problem then confronting the family. For example, consider the immemorial issue of parental favoritism among the children. The topic is easily broached when the concrete example of the relationship of Joseph and his brothers is used. The brothers were so enraged by paternal favoritism, as evidenced by his father's giving him the coat of many colors, that they contemplated Joseph's murder, though deciding finally to sell him into slavery. Raising the issue of sibling jealousy in this story is generally better than waiting until a child, in anger, makes an accusation. The Joseph story also permits a discussion not only of the origins of the claims of favoritism but the destructive consequences that may follow if the emotion is uncontrolled. Based on these discussions the parents may then adjust their own behavior to the child's legitimate criticisms. Parents also have the opportunity to give the children an explanation for what is presented as unfair treatment. A small modification in behavior by parent or child may lessen the intensity of feelings about favoritism.

The family will also develop a vocabulary for expressing feelings through these discussions. The next time the accusation about favoritism arises, the family will quickly recognize the syndrome merely by referring to the Joseph story. The discussion about the particular accusation will be further along just by the mere fact that parents and children will have in their mind a concrete example. Without the story, the parent and child are dealing with an abstract word to describe an emotion that is deeply felt but difficult to examine.

At the same time that the Torah discussion is giving the family a vocabulary for discussing family matters, the discussion is also providing the child with a vocabulary for dealing with religion. The view that children should be free to "choose" their own beliefs as they grow into adulthood is flawed. Children cannot make a choice if they do not have even the most basic vocabulary. The decision to keep a child's options open about religion by ignoring it is really a decision to avoid basing values upon any religious grounds.

Parents do not hesitate to instill numerous other values in the child's pattern of conduct. A parent firmly teaches a child to be law abiding. Being an outlaw is not an option. For many values we and our children are all heavily influenced by the popular culture. The issue of the day on television and in the newspapers is the one that sets the topics for discussion within our community and creates the political agenda at the various levels of government. If, for example, hallucinatory drugs are presented as having good uses in heightening awareness or making an individual more productive, then more permissive law enforcement results. A few years ago the cover of *Time* magazine (July 6, 1981) pictured a champagne glass to introduce an article on cocaine use in America. The inevitable association was that cocaine was socially sophisticated. A few years later, after persuasive evidence of the human destruction caused by cocaine, the same magazine (*Time*, April 11, 1983) had another article on cocaine. The cover featured an ominous picture. The cover and the article conveyed the uniform message that cocaine use leads to self-destruction.

Popular culture has many very attractive features that we accept wholeheartedly, like freedom, mobility, choice, and individual merit, but popular culture also has some features that do not embody constructive values.

Parents who expect that their children will acquire a pattern of values from them are usually actively involved in conveying their values. Thus, parents have the option to choose the principal ingredients of the culture they are imprinting upon their children, and they may decide what part of the popular culture to include along with the traditional values that have survived from generation to generation.

Parents may decline this challenge because they accept the popular culture as, by and large, embodying what they represent. Or, they may not believe that they have any option because the popular culture is so overwhelming.

The one option that is not available is the notion that the child will mature into adulthood and then have "freedom of choice" to decide upon whether to accept Jewish religious values. Without giving our children sufficient information and understanding of the values based on Jewish religious texts, the child may grow up attracted to a group with religious values that are at war with those of Jewish parents or be ignorant about the positive features of religion.

The prevailing culture creates ambivalent feelings about religion. Religious personalities are often presented as engaging in sugary goodness or as narrow-minded and potentially destructive. A catch phrase is that "religion is okay for people who need it." The statement suggests that religion is only for the naive, that it is not scientifically based, is divisive, and deals with arcane texts. The simple answer is that for approximately 100 generations serious people have studied and commented on the Torah. Among those who do so today, you will find individuals who have broad educations and who are actively involved in the world around them, with a life similar to yours.

As you will, your contemporaries who engage in Torah discussion are dealing with the difficult issues presented in the Torah. The questions that seem "unknowable" create discomfort. When you hear one, you will heave a mental sigh and invisibly shrug your shoulders, muttering to yourself, "Why am I being burdened with this question?" A question where few prospects exist for reaching a definitive answer may be a heavy intellectual burden. The perennially unanswerable questions include why the righteous or innocent suffer—the problem of the suffering of the innocent child.

The Torah also presents other scientifically unknowable and difficult subjects: angels, miracles, and the intervention of God in the affairs of man. Sometimes parents become afraid or paralyzed when first asked questions about the role of God. It need not be so. Answering these and similar questions does not require fabrication. The sages of Judaism had different answers to some of the same questions that will emerge at your family Torah discussions. Why did God make animals first, before he made Adam and Eve? Why did God destroy virtually all living things at the time of Noah? Why would God instruct Abraham to offer his son as a sacrifice?

Several ways exist to answer questions when you do not have your own response. One is to say simply that you do not have an answer and that the family should discuss how to resolve the issue. Another is to say, "I do not have the answer, but the tradition (or this commentator) has an answer that says. . . ."

For some circumstances the solutions are straightforward. A young child will probably not even raise difficult questions about supernatural or miraculous occurrences because young children accept these as easily as a "fact" of nature. An older child may express strong feelings about a particular passage, and a response is needed. However, recognition of the feeling itself may be sufficient if you do not have or do not wish to give a sophisticated, fact-based answer.

A fear of being labeled as a hypocrite should not deter you from the study of materials that require a temporary suspension of twentieth-century rationality or those that do not depict the highest standards of accepted morality. Serious Torah scholars experience intellectual tension when they read a part of the Torah that presents moral ambiguity. The conflict between reason, emotion, and faith is a perfectly natural response and need not create guilt or cynicism or result in avoiding the activity altogether. Without such a struggle, the family is deprived of acquiring the strength needed for struggles with other hard issues later.

Talking about hard Torah issues within a family eases the way for discussions on otherwise frightening issues like death and dying. The children know that their family permits what other families avoid. The parent and child are secure in the knowledge that no topics are too awesome to discuss. This enhances mutual feelings and lessens the child's fright about the unknowable questions of life itself.

Torah study is a challenge for each parent because tension between the world as we see it and the world depicted in the Torah is inevitable. Torah table talk will stimulate discomfort created by struggling with the unanswerable questions. You may discover, paradoxically, that conversations about the unknowable can create the most exciting and intimate parent-child exchanges.

We have not yet exhausted all the reasons for not engaging in family Torah talk. Some of the persons who attend the discussion may adversely affect it. Carried to the extreme, these personality types may be likened to the first three of the ten plagues that befell the Egyptians when they refused to permit the Israelites to leave slavery. The first plague was the pollution of the waters, when the waters turned to blood; the second, when frogs overran the land, intruding into every area of life; and the third plague, when lice attacked man and beast.

The first plague of family Torah discussion begins with the invited guest or family member who is determined to be glum and radiate boredom, like the polluted waters creeping through the land, thereby dampening everyone else's enthusiasm.

The second plague is frogs. This is an appropriate characterization for the impatient persons who immediately seek to change the discussion agenda and jump away from Torah discussion to some unrelated topic of mundane concern.

The third plague attacks every idea placed on the table for discussion. A professional cynic can come in and tear apart every idea. Given enough practice anyone can develop the scoffer's skills. The cynic is a person who has carried the healthy aspect of critical analysis to a destructive end. At the family dinner table we certainly cannot solve the reasons for these personality traits, but we can try to limit their corrosive effect. You might try to suggest that the discussion process you envisage does not provide for this systematic destruction. How and whether to say so to a guest is a matter of etiquette best dealt with by the leaders of the discussion.

Even members of the family who are not destructive can unintentionally affect the tenor of the discussion. You should be on guard for members of your extended family who are unwilling to enter into the spirit of Shabbat eve and lend encouragement to the family Torah discussion. Perhaps, if you take them aside and explain how important the discussions are to your family, they will accept the priorities you are setting and attend the family gathering on the accepted terms.

Certain problems may make the discussion difficult to conduct even where everyone has a positive attitude. For example, a single parent pursuing a job or career, managing the home, providing the food, and then attempting to lead the discussion has a formidable combination of responsibilities.

A negative attitude by one spouse may prevent the family discussion process from taking root. Thus, if one spouse wants to hold the discussion but the other is indifferent or antagonistic to the idea, the children will find all the support needed for withdrawing from the discussions.

For some families a discussion at the family dinner table is not the proper setting, but a discussion can occur at other times and other places. Whatever the time and place, establish a degree of intimacy within the family group. Placing everyone in the living room around the fireplace may create for one particular family the setting that is more likely to assure success than the suggested setting of Shabbat eve.

Going to another family's home where discussion has already taken root will quickly convey the right message and may itself serve as a model to establish the idea that Torah discussion occurs amongst people you know.

If, after all this, you are still having difficulty in starting the family Torah discussion process, then invite a family you know that is already engaged in the discussion process to come to your home so that you can get some on-the-job training as to how the discussion actually occurs. Inviting another family that is also involved in Torah discussion on a periodic basis can reinforce the idea in the children that Torah discussion appeals to others.

Others are available to assist you. The least conventional way is to place an advertisement in your local newspaper to see if you can attract other Jewish families who have the same idea for forming a family network to study together, which, in turn, will provide the basis for discussions within your home. A more conventional method is to use the Jewish educational facilities in your community. Your rabbi and synagogue may already have a program that can be used as the vehicle for bringing together parents who are undertaking family Torah discussion.

No matter where or what you learn outside the home, do not use your family discussion session merely as an opportunity to read from your notes. This will lead to a disaster. You must rethink what you learn in any formal session and present it for your own group. Most likely, the formal session will offer much more than your family can or should absorb in an evening.

If you do not have anyone to give you personal instruction, persevere, because some combination, such as the one we discuss hereafter, will eventually work for your family.

BREAK GLASS IN CASE OF FIRE

Do not read this unless you are unable to start the family discussion after using our other suggestions. If you are still having difficulty in starting the family Torah discussion process, then you may have to reach out to other resources. Join or create a network of several families with children that are or have embarked on family Torah discussion. The advantages of group involvement to solve problems is well known. You may recall the support you received from the group of expectant parents at childbirthing classes, where the parents-to-be, all at the same stage of life, discussed common concerns. The group probably had a leader who could answer technical questions, but the other participants provided the sounding board for the exchange of information. The class served its purpose within a few months. Thereafter, each participant was somewhat of an expert in advising others about the birthing process.

To create a group, start with that most powerful of information disseminators. Word of mouth is strong enough to establish the success or failure of multimillion-dollar movie productions, so surely it can help find the handful of persons for whom you are searching. Word of mouth is still a primary source of the information upon which people act, even in this age of instant electronic communications. Eventually, a few persons will hear that you are trying to organize a discussion group as support for family Torah discussion.

Our list of reasons for not engaging in Torah discussion ends here. None of the reasons given nor any that you can imagine is of such seriousness as to place you in physical or emotional jeopardy. Overcoming lingering reservations to engage in family Torah discussion means opening the door on bright possibilities.

A
CONTEMPORARY
REASON FOR
FAMILY TORAH
TALK

TORAH TALK AND THE
PSYCHOLOGY OF THE HEALTHY FAMILY

Torah table talk offers a structure to bring the family together regularly. This commitment builds into the family an internal support system. The family benefits from both the inherent values in the Torah and the derivative benefit of a stronger family support system. Everyone recognizes that the group depends on each individual's attendance and participation in order to survive and flourish. In time, family members develop a sense of being irreplaceable within the family group. The support system is important to help families manage the daily stresses and tensions. Child or adult, we all want someone to listen empathetically. A child comes home with pent-up feelings because a teacher has made unfair accusations about misconduct. An adult is upset at losing a business opportunity or merely from suffering rude comments in an insignificant encounter with a taxi driver. Each wants the opportunity to express these concerns. A support system is a place to try out new ideas without being ridiculed and to receive encouragement for accepting risks. It is a place to lick wounds. The support system can provide security because you know that you will not lose your membership in this group.

Ideally, the family can provide the best support system because it is ongoing—the individual and the family are together every day—and admission is established by blood or marriage. Family support groups are a contemporary version of the best features of an earlier generation's extended family: a way to get recognition or a helping hand, to find a person to confide in, or to receive a pat on the back.

The family is not the only support system. Individuals who come together regularly for any activities can form support systems, even if the initial reason for association was a common interest in a sport, gardening, or a business investment. People may come together based on a common status, like single parents or mothers of newborns. The support system will develop as long as that status or the common interest remains.

Obviously, Torah talk is not the only way to establish a

support system; nor is it the exclusive one even for families that engage in this activity. We recognize that the vast majority of family support systems are derived in other ways. Nonetheless, Torah talk has some unique qualities in that it develops a support system within the family, while easing entrance into a group that shares similar values. Torah discussion as the organizing principle of a support system is not dependent on age, physical agility, gender, or even educational achievement.

A support system based on a sports activity will wither when an arm loses its powers or a back gives out. Read the tearful farewells when a professional player reaches the end of his career. The pain of parting from his teammates is always what each says is the most difficult.

A family support system based on Torah talk has a common language, value system, and identity that cements relationships and provides security and friendship. When family members learn together and from each other on a regular basis, an enduring and well-grounded connection is formed. The idea of the necessity for a strong family support system contrasts with the "do your own thing" philosophy, which emphasizes the individual's quest for instant gratification and disregard of any group responsibility.

Family systems need supportive mechanisms for survival. Torah table talk is one that works. Torah table talk is a way to re-create the family—the original network—as a central source of nourishment. The activity will have the same effect in one-parent families, two-parent families, extended families, with young married couples, and with one-child, two-child, or no-child families. When you have guests participating at the Torah discussion you are sharing the experience, not diminishing it. In short, the rules for Torah discussion do not require a fixed number of players.

Torah table talk is not for the parent who wishes only to be heard and is not willing to listen. Instead, this process of conversation leads to communication among parents, children, and friends. The essence of the process is that each participant's observations have the potential for adding to the discussion. A five year old can raise a point that legitimately changes the direction of the conversation or adds another thought to the discussion. The older participants may have the principal responsibility for moving the discussion forward but each participant has accepted responsibility for adding a brushstroke to the conversational canvas. Viewed this way, the time together can be intensely alive, stimulating, and enjoyable—a time when no one can fail and each is satisfied.

Torah table talk nourishes the family in the three important ways a family must provide for a child:

1. Food for bodies,
2. Stimulating talk for the mind,
3. Encouragement for emotional freedom and positive self-concept.

1. Food for Bodies

Everyone recognizes the importance of eating together as a social force. The immediate image of a traditional Jewish meal would arise from merely saying "chicken soup." An Italian extended family group would meet around the pasta. A family around the turkey on Thanksgiving is part of the American iconography.

The value of the special atmosphere created by a meal should not be underestimated. For some, the essence of important personal occasions is the selection of a restaurant with appropriate atmosphere and cuisine. The selection of the restaurant is the act that expresses feelings for a spouse or close friends.

The special effort that goes into the preparation and serving of the Shabbat meal within the home introduces an occasion of importance. We use the finest china and silverware, those usually reserved for "events" when guests visit. We create a special feeling by the knowledge that our ancestors enjoyed the same traditional meal on Friday night as we enjoy each Shabbat and that Jews elsewhere are honoring the Shabbat in the same way. At that moment, the sweet savor of the meal gives meaning to the evening.

2. Stimulating Talk for the Mind

Torah table talk nourishes by stimulating intellectual development. Schools do not cultivate all of an individual's potential creativity. The defect of excessive passive learning is that a child may tend to accept too much of what is presented and not utilize curiosity to wrestle with an idea or fact that requires effort.

The goal in Torah table talk is just the opposite. Rather than teach in ways that may limit our children's learning, it uses reinforcing techniques and positive approaches that direct our children's full energy and intelligence toward creative, unique, and constructive thinking.

Torah table talk is not all talk and no action. The use of

drama and games as part of the Torah table talk should not be viewed as insignificant, either for the child or the parent. Learning a list of verb tenses or some other form of rote learning may involve an inevitable amount of drudgery. The majority of learning is inherently exciting and can retain that characteristic. A child may balk at learning the classical musical masterpieces but will gain enthusiasm for the piano through the gratification of playing a few popular tunes and then using that momentum to learn a Chopin piece.

The mind cannot be nourished where criticism is ever present. Criticism creates fear and destroys initiative. Criticism makes learning unpleasant, if not impossible. The fear of being wrong is a destructive force that inhibits learning and creates self-doubt, affecting the way a person looks at, deals with, and thinks about life. A scared child is always a poor learner. If a child is afraid of asking a question, commenting on a sentence, or interpreting a passage, afraid of displeasing parents or receiving humiliation in front of peers, the child will restrict learning to risk-free enterprises.

As a methodology, Torah table talk intends to encourage the opposite feelings about learning: to encourage good thinking habits and to strengthen the child's self-confidence. Children continually strive for information, and we as parents should exploit this natural inclination. Ultimately, we want our children to become people who love learning and know how to learn any subject.

Torah table talk teaches children how to solve problems. Torah often presents people in predicaments—problem situations. How they find their way out of these predicaments is the puzzle to present to our families for solutions. This problem-solving skill will apply to any situation the children face. The atmosphere for Torah table talk is one where mistakes are honorable and constructive rather than humiliating and where the most valuable gift we can give our children is to make the appropriate distinction. Parents have the perfect opportunity to show a positive feeling about learning on a weekly basis, during the Shabbat meal.

3. Encouragement of Emotional Freedom and Positive Self-Concept

A third form of nourishment provided by Torah table talk is emotional. Achieving a warm, trusting, and supportive relationship while maintaining a firm and instructive posture is a complex task, a universal struggle of all parents. Parenting is a challenge for us, as it was for Abraham, Isaac, and Jacob, or even Tevye in *Fiddler on the Roof*. We increase our chances for parental success by establishing a dialogue with our children, thus building emotional support systems for them.

Most parent-and-child conversations about values are necessitated by the child's misconduct. The most underdeveloped dialogue between parent and child is on the question of moral values. Typically, a parent confronts a child upon seeing or learning about a child's misbehavior. The child offers a defense. The parent becomes more outraged if the child is missing the moral point. Tempers flare. The parent screams and accuses the child of being morally obtuse. The child reacts in anger or shame or feels unjustly accused.

The entire episode, so familiar to any parent, leaves the child with a bad taste for discussing ethical conduct. The child focuses on the injustice of the parent's accusation or punishment, and the parent feels angry and disappointed with the child.

For the child, the learning of values may become associated only with negative experiences—a parent wagging a finger, sending a child to a room alone, or denying the child a trip to the movies or an amusement park. For the parent, these reprimands and denials to the child are legitimate forms of discipline. The raising of issues of conduct and values only in this context may lead to the child's rejection of any discussion about values. Our antidote is to have these discussions occur also when no family member is on trial for misconduct.

The family Torah conversation does not require a crisis as the starting bell. A calmer discussion on moral conduct is possible without any destructive effect. The weekly family conversation that focuses on moral conduct is not designed for reprimanding the child for misconduct. Indeed, the family must not use the discussion as an occasion for examining or reprimanding anyone's conduct. This would immediately turn the discussion into an occasion for attack and defense and unwittingly prove the point that discussions on moral conduct always result in strife. The purpose of the discussion is for parent and child to grapple together with the issues presented in the Torah, rather than for parent and child to grapple with each other.

Personal experiences may help illustrate the moral conduct under discussion. A parent or child may choose to share a personal experience or that of another to demonstrate praiseworthy conduct. A parent may find this occasion for offering praise to a spouse or child. The Torah text under discussion may bring to mind a personal predicament of a parent or child. Any participant may find the atmosphere at the discussion table sufficiently comfortable to raise personal predicaments, in order to get the perspective of the family.

The life predicaments of the Torah personalities may have the side benefit of permitting a participant at the discussion to better understand personal circumstances. A discussion about rivalry between brothers has its obvious counterpart in the brothers who are at the table. Their struggles with each other may not diminish just by having talked about an episode in the Torah. Nonetheless, their awareness of the struggles of other brothers, with sometimes dire consequences, may have a positive effect. The brothers at the dinner table may recognize that antagonistic feelings are not abnormal but that antagonistic feelings must be controlled. Without family discussion as a fixed routine, there is really no other natural occasion for such discussions.

THE TEN PRINCIPLES OF CHILD REARING

The traditional benefits of Torah table talk do not need any psychological justification. It is no coincidence, however, that family Torah talk contains all the features necessary to healthy growth and development in children. The National Institute of Mental Health has distilled the principles of child rearing into ten main categories.*

1. Love abundantly.
2. Discipline constructively.
3. Spend time together.
4. Tend to personal and marital needs.
5. Teach right from wrong.
6. Develop mutual respect.
7. Really listen.
8. Offer guidelines.
9. Foster independence.
10. Be realistic.

Plain Talk About Raising Children. National Institute of Mental Health, D.H.S. Publication No. (ADM) 81–875, 1979.

These are categories a parent may aspire to reach, with greater or lesser success. The key point is that some family activities are more likely to bring a parent closer to realizing these aspirations, while others have fewer possibilities. Family conversations on the Torah probably embody more of these characteristics than any other family activity. Taking a family trip is an occasion when some of these categories are fulfilled, but the family trip by its very nature does not have the regularity of weekly family discussion. The same is true of family outings to museums, sports events, camping, or shopping. Parent and child are together but the event itself may overwhelm the opportunity for discussion. Watching a television program or movie together may prompt a discussion on the depicted predicament. Usually, the viewing requires silence, and the time afterward is not always conducive to discussion. Though no doubt a healthy child can be developed in other ways and through the combination of the multitudinous events in which parents and children participate, when all is weighed, as a single activity regular family conversation on a topic of importance contains the highest percentage of essential ingredients to the development of a healthy child.

Ironically, the family Torah discussion permits the parents to use discipline in a constructive manner. Typically, parents must control a child's impulsive behavior by saying, "Don't do that." In regular family discussion, the child is affirmatively told to do something, to attend and participate in the family's Shabbat-eve discussion. The "do this" approach works better with children than the "don't do this." A regularized family practice has the encoded positive message: "Do" sit together as a family, "do" learn Torah, "do" enjoy traditional Jewish experiences like the Shabbat meal. Presenting activities in a positive manner is more likely to establish a positive feeling within the child than giving incessant negative statements and directions. The occasional negative comment will not erode the overall positive approach for disciplining the child.

The child learns not only from how a parent responds to each child in the family but also by closely observing the parent's general conduct. For example, a child will observe that the parent has accepted a discipline in preparing and conducting the Torah discussion. The child will note that the parent is meeting a self-imposed commitment, which the parent could easily find justification to forgo. Discipline is a theme that your family will inevitably discuss through some of the Torah studies.

Torah table talk must be geared for everyone sitting at the

dinner table. Child-centered Torah table talk, like child-centered-families, often produces neither happy children nor happy marriages. A discussion that makes the story childish will not appeal to adults and will soon lose its appeal to children. A mother and father who are enjoying Torah table talk are most apt to provoke similar feelings in their children. A complex story can be simplified without making it childlike. The moral predicament raised by the story should retain most of its complexity when presented to the children for their observations. The way to simplify the story yet retain its complexity is through the game approach we will suggest.

Family Torah discussion presents an unusually conducive setting for developing mutual respect among family members. Once each participant learns the guidelines for the conversation, none will have any difficulty in understanding what is to occur. Then, when the views of each child are encouraged and given sympathetic hearing, the child learns that youth is not bowing before age, nor is age abdicating to youth. Each person is a full participant. Parent and child usually have a more hierarchical relationship. A parent must ordinarily nudge the child to perform tasks required for the functioning of the family or the education of the child. With Torah talk, the regimen is quickly established and the child is brought in line only when disruption arises or the clearly understood boundaries are crossed.

Parents bring their knowledge base, interests, and talents to these family conversations. In turn, children are given a chance to discuss with their parents their different ideas and points of view openly and intelligently. The idea of respect for everyone at the table is stressed. Nevertheless, the well-conducted discussion never requires parents to forfeit control of the agenda, even when a child is recalcitrant about participating at the time.

Family Torah table talk will not ensure against all the ravages of contemporary life: failing marriages or children with problems. It can provide for every family a structure so that the whole of what is good about the family is not outweighed by the sum of its deficiencies. The fixed-time discussions will establish a routine of being together with learning as a common enterprise and serve as a regular reminder to all family members of how important each is to the others. Thus, family Torah talk may counter the divisive and alienating forces that cause family havoc by providing a regular forum for dialogue about important matters in a moral context.

UNDERSTANDING THE MORAL DEVELOPMENT OF YOUR CHILD

Does regular discussion about stories that raise moral issues have any effect on the moral development of the child? Many families do not engage in these discussions, yet their children appear to grow up as moral human beings. No definitive answer exists.

Psychologists Sigmund Freud and B. F. Skinner stressed the view that children learn most from their surroundings. For Freud, the major portion of the value system ultimately adopted by an individual was the one presented by the social environment: the impact of the closest persons during childhood and adolescence. The individual is confronted by competing values that may cause psychological strife before a dominant value system emerges. For Skinner, moral behavior is shaped by reinforcements. A child receives reinforcements, in varying degrees, to act or refrain from acting. Both of these approaches underscore the importance of the socialization process on the development of moral behavior. Family Torah discussion, with its emphasis on parents showing the way, is compatible with the theories of either Freud or Skinner.

Another perspective is that moral values are learned intuitively, springing from the internal nature of the person.* Others suggest that moral development parallels the maturation process of the normal child. A child develops progressively through each stage and level. In this view, children go through at least two and possibly more developmental levels, with different stages in each level. These stages emerge gradually.†

If that is so, does talking about moral development speed up the process or make the experience at each stage more complete? Is moral development like the study of mathematics, where each stage of accomplishment is dependent on mastery of a previous one?

Discussions about morals based on the appropriate developmental level of the child should encourage moral understanding, according to some theorists. The problem solving that arises

---

*Carol Gilligan, _In a Different Voice._ Cambridge, MA: Harvard University Press, 1982.

†Herbert Ginsberg and Sylvia Opper, _Piaget's Theory of Intellectual Development._ Englewood Cliffs, NJ: Prentice-Hall, Inc., 1969; Lawrence Kohlberg, _The Philosophy of Moral Development._ New York: Harper and Row, Inc., 1981.

from family discussions with the presentation of ideals of conduct should enhance and accelerate the moral development of the child and possibly even affect the adult participants.

At the very least, discussions about moral values provide a vocabulary for thinking and communicating on the issues. Even for those who argue that moral conduct is intuitive, an intuitive judgment is nurtured by the learning process. Some judgments made on a "gut reaction" are often the culmination of years of working with similar problems. In effect, the brain is programmed to make seemingly effortless judgments. Torah talk deals with an endless variety of complex situations and provides reasons for later "intuitive" judgments on how to act in a given circumstance.

Whatever the basis for judgments at any age level, a parent who is leading a family Torah discussion may sometimes be taken aback by the nature and type of a child's response. Do not despair or look aghast, for the child's answer is probably natural for his or her age.

Take the classic story about "the hole in the dress," described by the famous Swiss psychologist, Jean Piaget.* A little girl named Marie wanted to give her mother a nice surprise and cut out a piece of sewing for her. Unable to handle the scissors, she cut a big hole in her own dress.

Another little girl, Margaret, took her mother's scissors when her mother was out. She played with them, and then because she did not know how to use the scissors, she cut a small hole in her own dress while playing.

Two other children were asked which child, Marie or Margaret, should be punished more severely. The six year old responded that the one who made the larger hole should be punished. The twelve year old said that the one who was playing with the scissors without intending to help the mother should be punished. The six year old's response was typical of the developmental stage in which acts are judged by the material consequences. The twelve year old was able to consider the intention of the children in using the scissors and did not consider the size of the holes each made. No amount of explanation would have persuaded the six year old that there were at least two ways of looking at the situation. She was unable to entertain alternatives. The twelve year old was probably surprised at the reason-

---

*Jean Piaget, *The Moral Judgement of the Child*. New York: Free Press, 1965.

ing of the younger child and probably would not even remember giving a similar type of response when she was younger.

Recognition of these age-level distinctions will keep parental expectations realistic, contribute to the appropriate level of topic selection, and minimize the risk that the conversation will be under or over the child's head. When you have children of different age levels present, you may try to tailor the questions posed to each child. You will eventually recognize each child's level by the responses and know automatically how to proceed in the next round of discussion.

Indeed, you may find that an additional fascination of family Torah talk is testing your observations against those of the psychological theoreticians. Harvard Professor Lawrence Kohlberg has developed a three-level, six-stage moral development approach based on the theories of Piaget. We will sketch the six stages.

The Kohlberg six stages of moral development are logically ordered, each stage leading to the next. This progression of development is similar to learning about numbers: counting leads to arithmetic, then to algebra, and so on. So too Kohlberg asserts that children move from lower to higher stages of moral thought and cannot skip an intermediate stage. A child's moral view will not skip about to a higher stage and then back to a lower, but will predictably stay close to its developmental level.

Stage 1. (The punishment-and-obedience orientation.) A child will determine what is "right" by literal obedience to authority.

A child will avoid breaking rules, especially where there is expectation of punishment for breaking rules. The child's only interest is to avoid physical punishment. The child does not care about the effect on others of the questioned conduct.

Stage 2. (The personal fairness orientation.) A child will more likely follow rules if following the rule serves an immediate interest.

A child begins to see what constitutes an equal exchange, what is "fair" for the child and for others.

Stage 3. (The good boy–nice girl orientation.) A child begins to see what is appropriate conduct in relationship to what others regard as right conduct.

The child is now involved in mutual relationships of trusting one another, having respect for others. Concern about other persons, often peers, is developing. The child considers the expectations of the immediate family and friends.

Stage 4. (The "law and order" orientation.) A child now sees that actions should have some relationship to upholding a broader social order, beyond that of immediate relationships.

Now, the expectations of the larger society become more significant in affecting the child's conduct. Laws are upheld because they provide for the social order.

Stage 5. (The social contract, legalistic orientation.) A teenager may now evaluate most moral questions from the perspective of "the greatest good for the greatest number of people."

These rules should be upheld because they are part of a social contract among members of society at large.

Stage 6. (The universal–ethical principle orientation.) A person will consider problems in the context of abstract universal principles, which govern all of humanity.

Carol Gilligan takes issue with the general applicability of Kohlberg's stages of moral development. According to Gilligan, female moral development is unlike that of males because of the differences inherent in their biological compositions and social experiences. Kohlberg's research was limited to young males, and he therefore missed the distinctive themes in the moral development of women.

According to Gilligan, the morally mature woman may tend to approach moral issues based on an interpersonal sense of justice, arising from relationships with other people. By contrast, morally mature men are judged to have reached the highest stage of moral development when they demonstrate an abstract sense of justice, focused on rules and legislation. Women may thus appear to have only reached a third stage of moral development, measured by Kohlberg's stages. To Gilligan, the women are no less morally conscious human beings than the men who are apparently at Kohlberg's fifth or sixth stage.

We use Kohlberg's six stages not to suggest that this concept is the final word on this complex subject but because it provides a general framework for charting the moral development of our children.

Kohlberg's observations may pose special problems when viewed through the traditional perspective of Judaism. Kohlberg writes that in Stage 6 "Right is defined by the decision of conscience in accord with self-chosen ethical principles appealing to logical comprehensiveness, universality, and consistency. These principles are abstract and ethical (the Golden Rule, the categorical imperative); they are not concrete moral rules like the Ten Commandments. At heart, these are universal principles of justice, of the reciprocity and equality of human rights, and of respect for the dignity of human beings as individual persons."

One recent author has suggested that Kohlberg's view on moral development is in the main quite consistent with views expressed by some of the great Jewish sages: Maimonides, Rabbi Saadya Gaon, and others. Before suggesting these similarities, we will describe a hypothetical family discussion, which may help your assessments at the family Torah discussion.

Imagine a family with children at various developmental stages. The family has the unique custom of calling each child by its age. Seated around the table are Father, Mother, and the children named Four, Eight, and Fourteen. The family is discussing the Binding of Isaac, the episode where Abraham is told by God to bring his beloved son Isaac to Mount Moriah as a sacrificial offering. At the instant before Isaac is to die at the hand of his father, an angel appears and orders a halt. A sacrificial ram is substituted as the offering to God. (VaYera, Genesis 22:1–19)

Four's response is determined by literal obedience to the rules. Four says that it is wrong to kill. Or, Four may say that Abraham must follow God's command.

Mother then states that in antiquity human sacrifice existed. Eight comments that Abraham may have thought that God wanted human sacrifice. Abraham was willing to sacrifice his son so that God would have a good opinion of him. If human sacrifice was commonly practiced, then Abraham would not suffer any punishment from his neighbors for killing his son in this manner. Eight's analysis is based on what will happen to Abraham from those who can hold him accountable: God and the neighbors.

Fourteen now bursts forth and heatedly exclaims that local rules and customs do not matter. Unjustified killing is wrong under any circumstances. Fourteen heatedly states that the Nazis had laws that justified the deaths of millions of Jews. To confirm his opinion about a higher morality, Fourteen states that God did not permit the killing of Isaac. Fourteen is trying out a newly developed sense of universal ethical principles. No situational ethics for him.

Father's concluding observation is to point out the difficulty of having absolute faith in the rightness of a course of conduct. Father notes how difficult it is to act when the proposed conduct seemingly conflicts with other values. Mother then comments to Father, noting that Soren Kierkegaard's *Fear and Trembling*, a book by a nineteenth-century Danish Protestant minister,* developed the thesis that Abraham is the prototype for the man of faith.

Faith actually plays a role in the thinking of Kohlberg. He has stated that what he regards as the highest level of moral development, the universal stage of concern, is generally reached only by persons motivated by religious faith.

Kohlberg also states that the individual can develop through the six stages of moral development without necessarily putting those principles into action. He suggests that the leap from a higher level of moral understanding to the implementation in actual conduct is generally more evident among persons with a strong religious base.

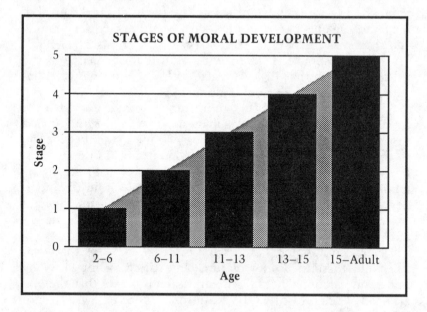

*Garden City, NY: Doubleday, 1954.

A comparison was recently made between the views of Kohlberg the contemporary psychologist and Maimonides, one of the greatest of Jewish sages, who lived 800 years ago. The conclusion of the author was that these two agree in significant measure.

1. Reasoning is an essential part of moral behavior.
2. Human beings pass through stages of moral development.
3. There is *some* correspondence between *age* and *stage*.
4. The thrust of moral development is *from* physical rewards, *through* "good roles," to "principled behavior."*

The instinct to "do the right thing" is not easily translated into action in a specific instance. Jewish tradition has a concept of mitzvot, proper conduct, arising from the Torah. Jewish law, the Halacha, has extensive prescriptions that are a commitment to a set of values and a way of conduct. The Jewish tradition is grounded in the idea that study of what is required conduct will lead to actions based on the requirements. The point is summarized in a brief incident among the rabbis.

> When Rabbi Tarfon and the sages were dining in the upper chamber of the house of Nitzah in Lydda, this question was asked of them: "What is greater, study or practice?" Rabbi Tarfon answered, "Practice is greater." Rabbi Akiba answered, "Study is greater." Then all the sages said, "Study is greater because study leads to practice."†

---

*Earl Schwartz, *Moral Development: A Practical Guide to Jewish Teachers.* Denver: Alternatives in Religious Education, Inc., 1983, pp. 14–15.

†Ibid., p. 15.

TRADITIONAL TEXT, UNCONVENTIONAL APPROACH

THE TEN UNIVERSAL QUESTIONS

Fire! Fire! You have ten minutes to prepare for a family Torah discussion. The persons who will participate are already in the next room. A grandparent is tickling the youngest child, who is roaring with laughter. This week you did not have a moment free and were unable to prepare. The pressure mounts, because you are determined to have the weekly discussion. What to do? The ten universal questions to the rescue.

These questions focus on facts, action, and characters. They are the universal way of defining a topic, organizing thinking, starting or continuing a conversation, and stimulating imagination. A question takes us into the lives and experiences of others. These feelings, sensations, thoughts, and actions of individual personalities help us to understand the guiding ethical principles that govern their conduct. From this understanding we may modify our own guiding principles, strengthening those we already have or adding to those we had not previously confronted.

A universal question is relevant in any discussion of the Torah, but it is not the only way to conduct a Torah discussion.

The ten universal questions are:

1. What is the predicament?
2. Who is in the predicament?
3. What is the relationship between the people?
4. How is God involved?
5. How is the predicament resolved?
6. How does the community affect the predicament?
7. Does the predicament illuminate our contemporary life?
8. What ethical and moral principles are posed by the manner in which the predicament occurs or is resolved?
9. Does individual "free will" permit any other course of conduct?
10. How can you retell the story?

To demonstrate the universality of the questions we will take an incident in the Torah, apply the universal questions, and demonstrate their usefulness whether you discuss interpersonal struggles or social and political struggles.

The Story of Tzelafchad's Daughters

A petition was presented by the daughters of Tzelafchad, son of Chefer, son of Gilead, son of Makhir, son of Manasseh, of the family of Joseph's son Manasseh. The names of these daughters were Machlah, No'ah, Chaglah, Milkah, and Tirtzah. They now stood before Moses, Eleazar the priest, the princes, and the entire community at the Communion Tent entrance with the following petition:

"Our father died in the desert. He was not among the members of Korach's party who protested against God, but he died because of his own sin without leaving any sons. Why should our father's name be disadvantaged in his family merely because he did not have a son? Give us a portion of land along with our father's brothers."

Moses brought their case before God.

God spoke to Moses, saying:

"The daughters of Tzelafchad have a just claim. Give them a hereditary portion of land alongside their father's brothers. Let their father's hereditary property thus pass over to them.

"Speak to the Israelites and tell them that if a man dies and has no son, his hereditary property shall pass over to his daughter. If he has no daughter, then his hereditary property shall be given to his brothers. If he has no brothers, you shall give his property to his father's brothers. If his father had no brothers, then you shall give his property to the closest relative in his family, who shall then be his heir."

This was the decreed law for the Israelites, as God had commanded Moses. (Pinchas, Numbers 27:1–11)

The tribes protested God's decision to award the inheritance to Tzelafchad's daughters, saying: "But if they [the daughters] marry a member of another Israelite tribe, then the hereditary property coming to us from our fathers will be diminished, since it will be added to the tribe into which they marry. Our hereditary property from the lottery system will thus be diminished." (Massey, Numbers 36:3)

Moses gave the Israelites instructions at God's command, saying, "The tribe of Joseph's descendants have a just claim. This is the word that God has commanded regarding

Tzelafchad's daughters: You may marry anyone you wish
as long as you marry within your father's tribe. The
hereditary property of the Israelites will thus not
be transferred from one tribe to another, and each person
among the Israelites will remain attached to the hereditary
property of his father's tribe." (Massey, Numbers 36:5–7)

1. Who is in the predicament? The five daughters of Tzelafchad: Machlah, No'ah, Chaglah, Milkah, and Tirtzah; also, Moses, Eleazar the priest, the princes, and the entire community.

2. What is the predicament? The daughters are challenging the
inequity of the proposed distribution of land among the sons of
the tribes and the exclusion of female inheritance.

3. What is the relationship between the people? Their father
Tzelafchad was a descendant of Manasseh, the son of Joseph.
While each of Joseph's eleven brothers formed a separate tribe,
Joseph's was especially recognized. Instead of the creation of a
single tribe of Joseph, two half tribes were formed by his sons,
Ephraim and Manasseh.

4. Is God involved? God decides the merits of the claim and
gives precise instructions on inheritance laws among the Israelites.

5. How is the predicament resolved? Through God's intervention.

6. How does the community affect the predicament? The community, the elders of the tribe of Manasseh, requests and receives an amendment to God's ruling that daughters are
permitted to inherit land. Daughters are permitted to inherit land
only if they marry a man within their tribe, thereby avoiding the
possibility that the land would go to a member of another tribe.
The latter would occur if the daughters married men from other
tribes, and their children, taking their father's tribal affiliation,
would own land that once belonged to Manasseh and is within
its territorial boundaries. The community interest is a strong
element of the resolution of the predicament. (Massey, Numbers
36:1–12)

7. Does the predicament illuminate our contemporary life? At
its most obvious level, this story deals with distinctions made on

the basis of gender; also, the process of making a moral argument as a reason for changing a law. A law may on the whole be good, but in its application in particular unanticipated circumstances may have consequences that are unjust.

8. What ethical and moral principles are posed by the manner in which the predicament occurred or is resolved? The community is dealing with its moral obligation to the individual. A person who is aggrieved may petition for a consideration of her rights. The daughters do not evidence any fear or need of restraint in challenging the proposed conduct of Moses and the other leaders.

The daughters effectively present a petition for personal justice. They argue that the community's land distribution limited to male heirs will be disadvantageous to their family line. They acknowledge that sinful conduct by a father can cause a loss of the inheritance and distinguish between sins that might justify disinheritance and sins that do not.

Rebellion against God may justifiably cause disinheritance to the family line.

The daughters do admit that their father committed a personal sin, which caused his death. The community appears aware of the circumstances of the father's death, although it is not described in the episode. A personal sin is apparently not the basis for disallowing an inheritance for sons. Therefore, the daughters argue that their father's sin and resulting death should not disinherit them. The only reason for disinheriting them is because they are women, and this they challenge. God hears them and commands a general rule to include women within the rights of inheritance.

9. Does the individual "free will" permit any other course of conduct? The women had the choice of accepting or challenging the custom of the community. We do not know how Moses and the leaders would have resolved the issue, because Moses brought the issue to God.

10. How can you retell the story? The daughters' petition to Moses and the elders is similar to persuading a legislature to change a law that is having unjust results. Assign participants to serve as the principal characters. Hold hearings to discuss reasons for the existing law and the requested changes.

Commentary on the Ten Universal Questions

The use of the ten universal questions may be enhanced by considering their definitions and the additional inquiries they provoke.

1. *Who is in the predicament?* A participant in the predicament is any person whose actions or mere existence influences the outcome of the predicament. Also, any person who is affected by the outcome is in the predicament.

What seems to motivate them? How do we understand their roles as well as their personalities? Do you identify with any of them or would you like to be like one of them? What feelings does each personality evoke in you?

2. *What is the predicament?* A predicament describes a tug of war between personalities. A predicament is both self-contained and connected to the preceding events.

What background information do we need either on a personality or the situation? What happened immediately before the story that may have contributed to the predicament? What can we expect to happen as a result of the episode?

3. *What is the relationship between the people?* A relationship is the family tie that describes the ancestors and descendants of the principal characters. A family tie is a prologue to any individual's story. A family tie may clarify the motivations of an individual within a predicament.

How are the family linkages powerful forces in the lives of the characters? Who are the characters' parents and grandparents? What types of relationships developed with siblings, with parents, and with God?

How do the persons feel about one another? What emotions are they revealing? Joseph wept aloud when he reconciled with his brothers. Moses was angry when the Israelites created the golden calf. The feelings of the characters enhance the meaning.

4. *How is God involved?* The involvement of God is through direct communication with an individual or through direct intervention in the life of a person or people. Any intervention by God underscores the importance of an individual and the event.

How is God communicating? Sometimes he communicates

through the image of the burning bush, elsewhere by a moving cloud. When God gives instructions does He give commands or engage in dialogue? What demands does God make on the people? Do people react to God's actions? When He does punish, why does He? When and why does God intervene with supernatural powers?

5. *How is the predicament resolved?* A predicament is resolved by the actions that settle the specific problem.

The Torah generally describes how a predicament is resolved. Individuals are not left hanging from a tree stump at the edge of a cliff overlooking a canyon without any obvious prospect for rescue. You will know how a story ends.

You may or may not know why a particular ending occurred. Is the predicament resolved through the actions of one of the characters or by God?

Pharoah's refusal to permit the Israelites to leave Egypt is a classic example of ambiguity. God hurled plagues against Egypt but Pharaoh adamantly refused to permit the Israelites to leave despite the havoc wrought in his country. The Torah states, "Pharaoh hardened his heart and did not let the Israelites leave, just as God had predicted through Moses." (VaEra, Exodus 9:35) Why and how this occurred has been a continuing subject of discussion throughout the centuries.

6. *How does the community affect the predicament?* A community affects a predicament by cultural habits, beliefs, expectations, and leadership.

What is the community's social and political structure? How did things "get done"? The society's complexity is suggested by the types of goods manufactured. What are the available resources? What is sown and harvested? What is the individual's relationship to the land? What do people do for a living? How do the types of occupations provide information about the community? Is an individual's occupation somehow suggestive of the character of a person?

7. *Does the predicament illuminate our contemporary life?* A predicament illuminates contemporary life if it will either enhance your life or lessen the effect of undesirable consequences.

How have you reacted in the same type of predicament? Have you experienced similar emotions? Are you surprised by the resolution of the predicament? Why is this the resolution of the predicament in the Torah?

8. What ethical and moral principles are posed by how the predicament occurs or is resolved? An ethical or moral principle is posed when an action may harm or benefit another person.

What effect does the action have on another person? Is the effect harmful or beneficial? What is the effect of the action in God's sight? Under what circumstances does a third party who is not in the predicament have an obligation to intervene? May the third party avoid intervention where high personal risk exists?

9. Does individual "free will" permit any other course of conduct? "Free will" means that an individual can make choices in how to act. The absence of free will means that the individual is an actor in a play where the script is written and no individual choice is permitted. Everything happens because it could not happen otherwise.

Could the person choose to act otherwise? If so, why was this action taken? Does God permit a person to act contrary to his command? If so, what are the consequences of exercising free will contrary to God's command?

10. How can you retell the story? Telling a story in a different form gives an appreciation of details that are not otherwise evident. The game approach suggests different ways to retell a story. Not every game suggested is suitable to each story.

A dramatic reenactment is a good way to retell a story with characters whose actions involve challenge or struggle.

What point do you want to emphasize? Which retelling format best simplifies a complex predicament? How do you choose a retelling format for the allotted time? Which retelling format is the most suitable for involving your participants?

The most famous questions in the Jewish tradition are the four asked each year by the youngest child at the Passover seder. The ten universal questions do not have the drama associated with those, but they are a sure way of getting a family into the drama of the Torah.

DRAMA TEACHES RATHER THAN PREACHES

The traditional way of study among Jews is an intense intellectual experience between a scholar and his disciples. Hazy photographs depict a long, wooden, rickety table. Men or young boys with the layered look, bundled up against the damp cold of the somber interior, sit on a narrow bench with each pressing against his seatmate. A rabbi dressed in black with a white beard and covered head rhythmically reads from an oversized book. Everyone is looking at the text, some from the sides, others with an upside-down view. No one's mind is allowed to wander as the text is quoted, questioned, explained, and answered. Discipline is enforced. The pedagogical technique worked in its time and place and still continues in many places, with a few adaptations.

For the family unaccustomed to the traditional mode of teaching, a different pedagogical technique will build a bridge to the past. Drama is a perfect vehicle to build enthusiasm for the study.

Drama has impact. Acting out a small part of the Torah is not going to give the actors a full understanding of the text, but the play will give much more than merely a sketchy retelling of the narrative. After experiencing the story through the play, the child and the parent can discuss the text.

Children are enthusiastic about role playing because the activity has the pure pleasure of play without the obvious discipline required in more formal learning. The freedom to create and expand the role adds to the enjoyment for both child and parent. Once started, a child is reluctant to stop, even when the presentation has ended.

To construct a drama for the entire family begin by telling what you plan to do. This reduces anxiety and motivates participation.

> Tonight we are going to learn a story from the Torah. We will act out a story; everyone will have a role. Listen to the story, so we can decide what character you will assume. When we finish the story, you will tell me who you want to be. Children get the first chance at choosing a role, and assignments will then be made to as many adults as necessary.

Give a one-minute synopsis. Later, as the play unfolds, a parent can keep the context clear when the children are actually experiencing the personalities of the characters. For the moment, help each person to select a role, keeping in mind that young children may need quick guidance so that they are not delayed in choosing among competing attractions. The children often choose a sympathetic character or one who conveys power and importance. Nonetheless, children and adults enjoy improbable assignments, such as an adult who takes the role of a child and a youngster who becomes the king or pharaoh. Some of the important personalities may not have much to say in a particular setting, a perfect role for the youngest child who can then feel important, yet not frustrated by the assignment. Parental intervention to guide a young child along in the role is welcomed both by the child and by the other participants, who become impatient when delayed. The parent should be positioned near the younger children so that the intervention is not obtrusive.

Children of ten years of age and older can become the directors of the show. Merely suggest that the children go for no more than a five-minute discussion to plan the story and then return to tell everyone how the story will evolve. Above all, the play must begin, sooner rather than later.

Very simple props enhance the story, especially those that rely on imagination. Use a spoon as a sword, a bathrobe for royal robes, a stick for a staff, a hat for a crown, or a nightgown for a queen. The family can quickly brainstorm as to appropriate props, and a child can then rush enthusiastically to find the needed items.

This enthusiasm of the children will help some of the adults relax and join in the spirit of the occasion. Laughter and joy can not only release tension but can also build memories between people. Your children will remember these moments in their own old age. Laughter is ageless.

A skeptic may doubt whether any significant learning can occur amidst laughter and whether this treatment of stories from sacred texts is appropriate. Separate the high spirits of the acting from the message of the Torah. The dramatic enactment is designed to give children a quick understanding of the facts and issues.

A complex and seemingly uninteresting issue can be quickly and entertainingly conveyed through a skit. Act out a scene in which one child takes the role of a person about to leave on a trip who goes to a neighbor to leave a valuable article of silver. When he returns from the trip, the neighbor advises him that the item is not available. Who must accept the consequences of the loss? (Mishpatim, Exodus 22:6–8) The children may overact the skit, but the discussion about responsibility for entrusted goods is serious learning. They will have a basis for discussing whether it matters if the goods are lost due to negligence or theft. Does it matter whether you paid the neighbor for safeguarding the goods or were merely asking for a favor? This skit gives everyone a quick and understandable common factual basis for a leap into a Torah discussion on the laws governing responsibility where one entrusts property to another. At first, this appears to be an extremely dry topic for a family discussion. However, once having taken part in the skit, each child has made an investment and will make a commitment to listen and learn about the significance of what has transpired.

Drama incorporates many of the cognitive skills of traditional learning situations. The skills of sequencing, categorizing, memorizing, abstracting, and generalizing information are all incorporated into the dramatic experience.

The magical quality of drama invites our imagination to soar. We can be strong, fearless, powerful, and daring. In the world of pretend, we can think or control anyone. We can feel a sense of freedom and importance that may not be available in everyday living. The smallest child in the family can be anointed the king or pharoah, the most articulate child in the family can become Aaron, the spokesperson for Moses, and a child who wonders about her physical appearance can become Rachel, a beautiful woman. This is a perfect opportunity for everyone to feel good. There is no room for judgment or critical comments. The participants are not responsible for the outcome of the story. They are responsible only for where imagination will take them.

Finally, the children are learning not only from their own participation but from that of their parents. The adults, by taking part in the skit, are demonstrating that occasional falling down, not getting it right, and taking on of roles inconsistent with expected behavior is part of taking chances, a desirable character quality.

Dramatic presentations within the family and the discussion that follows are an exceptional opportunity for a child to become comfortable in speaking with both adults and peers. Practice at expressing throughts to a group leads to general comfort in making public presentations, an always valuable skill and one that makes for a more attractive personality.

As for teenagers, what could be more valuable than a regularly scheduled opportunity to express strongly held views that are independent of their parents? The teenagers have the freedom to express the negative feelings hidden away in the secret corners of their minds. For instance, a child who has a difficult time with a teacher may select a role to play that expresses anger at authority. The roles that are chosen and how they are played may send signals or may, at the least, permit the expression of anger in nondestructive ways through role playing. A caution is that these feelings may also be exaggerated because of the very nature of the dramatic exercise, to pretend.

The expression of negative feelings will not necessarily erase the feelings or alter drastically the behavior of children or adults. You may, on the other hand, also be amazed to find the expression of positive feelings that you did not know existed. The expression of feelings through the structure of Torah table talk drama may aid family communication.

Within drama a child or an adult is given a safe place to express himself or herself. Go ahead, raise the curtain.

LIGHTS, CAMERA, ACTION

Man, woman, or child, you quickly build enthusiasm for learning Torah if you "game-play" the topic you have chosen for the weekly discussion. You will bring alive the characters you are going to discuss by taking a role, working with other "actors," and placing yourself on the stage of your dining room with other family members. Game playing works whether you are going line by line, with each weekly portion, or through the great themes. Game playing is a form of dramatic presentation that is especially well suited for family Torah talk.

Game playing can be a serious business. Military experts and diplomats regularly conduct crisis management games to determine how to react if a real crisis occurs. What should the United States do if a Soviet–Cuban supported uprising occurs in Mexico? Game playing requires participants to take their roles seriously. If you are assigned the role of the Soviet leader, then you must consider how to overcome the distance from Mexico and how you will react to American counteractions. The American leadership has the other side of the equation: Mexico is close, but so are the millions of people who would seek to cross the border in search of haven in the United States. The person playing the role of secretary of state must take into account whether or how we would react to masses of refugees streaming across the Rio

Grande to the southwestern deserts. The solution to these problems is limited by the possible alternatives.

Realistic solutions to the game playing are encouraged, rather than magical ones. A magical solution is easy and is essentially meaningless because the proponent merely waves the wand and solves the problem. A realistic solution requires dealing with hard choices. The final decision is subject to examination by the other game players.

Parents encourage game playing because, ironically, it teaches children to think about situations realistically. Take Monopoly. The primary value of the game is not in teaching the children about real estate. Though they do learn a few terms that are not generally in a child's world—buying and selling property, mortgaging to obtain loans for construction, having creditors and being a debtor—the game does not teach them about real estate syndication principles or how to form tax shelters or become successful developers.

The instructive value of Monopoly and every game is to place each child in a situation where the child's decisions have consequences. Moreover, the child learns that the outcome may be affected by the decisions of others or by chance occurrences.

Game playing is used universally to evaluate one side's skill against the others and to account for the role of chance. Trial lawyers engage in exhaustive examinations of their clients to demonstrate how opposing counsel will conduct cross-examination. Business executives engage in this process to explore how competitors will act under given circumstances. If we introduce a new product at a fixed price, how will our competitors respond? What if the price is 20 percent higher?

Game playing is no less real for the family Torah discussion. The rules of game playing are:

1. Each participant agrees for the moment to give up personal identity, including inhibitions.
2. Each participant agrees to assume wholeheartedly the role of the assigned character.
3. The role of the assigned character requires understanding of the character's interests and goals in the given situation.
4. Each character must under these circumstances respond realistically to the other characters and the situation.

The benefits of game playing include:

1. Giving all participants a common understanding of the facts; and
2. Exploring complex situations in a manageable manner.

You are "making points" as you proceed through these games but there is no scorekeeper, no winners or losers. A point is scored when you locate a moral value embedded in the story. The points emerge as the game is played. As you read a particular text, choose a game to focus the family's attention on the occurrence you intend to discuss. The central objective is for all to understand the text, not to play a particular type of game. You may eventually decide to design different games more suited to your interests, the personalities and ages within your family, and the text under discussion.

We suggest you read about each type of game. We also suggest texts appropriate to treatment within a particular game structure. You may choose only to scan the examples briefly, coming back later when you are either reading the specific text in your family discussion, deciding on which approach to use, or designing your own game.

The concluding portions of this chapter contain ideas for hands-on construction. An adventuresome family with latent construction skills may undertake the complex task of building models of sacred objects according to the specific instructions given in the Torah.

By contrast, everyone can engage in the straight dramatization of a Torah narrative. The play will often spring off the pages of the text. You will not need a script writer. Nonetheless, we offer a few suggestions to get a family started on what can become a regular and eagerly anticipated standing-room-only show.

We offer almost twenty ideas for different types of games along with multiple examples as to how each game may be played. Scan a few now. You need not read all of them at one time because they are not intended to be read straight through. The examples in the Table of Games were selected to highlight the key features of the game. Our sequence of Torah portions is not that of the Torah itself.

Use the Table of Games when you are reading one of the Torah portions that we have used as an example. Or, use the Table of Games to suggest how you can approach any Torah portion you wish to discuss, even if we do not discuss it among our examples.

Table of Games

1. **Editorial**
   Adam and Eve (Bereshith, Genesis 2:15–3:20)
2. **The Courtroom Game**
   Jacob and Esau (Toledoth, Genesis 27:1–19)
   Adam and Eve and the Serpent (Bereshith, Genesis 2:15–3:20)
   Aaron and the Golden Calf (Ki Thisa, Exodus 32:1–35)
3. **Game of the Highest Stakes: Between God and Man**
   Destruction of Sodom (VaYera, Genesis 18:20, 23–33)
   Moses and the Aftermath of the Golden Calf (Ki Thisa, Exodus 32:7–14)
4. **International Diplomacy**
   Envoys to the Edomites (Chukath, Numbers 20:14–21)
   King of Arad Chooses War (Chukath, Numbers 21:1–3)
   Balak and Balam, the Impact of Alliances (Balak, Numbers 22:2–25)
5. **Intelligence Gathering**
   The Mission of the Spies to Canaan (Sh'lach 24:25, Numbers 13:17–20)
   Pharaoh and the Hebrew Midwives (Shemoth, Exodus 1:17–19)
6. **The Media**
   Egypt Pursues Israelites (BeShalach, Exodus 14:2–10)
   The Ten Plagues (VaEra, Exodus 7:26–8:11)
   The Departure of the Israelites from Egypt (Bo, Exodus 11:1–13:16)
7. **Reordering of Events**
   Creation (Bereshith, Genesis 1:1–2:3)
   The Ten Plagues (VaEra-Bo, Exodus 7:14–11:8)
8. **The Social Scientist Conducting Exit Poll**
   The Going Forth from Egypt (Shemoth, Exodus)
9. **Crisis Management**
   Joseph Preparing for the Famine (MiKetz, Genesis 41:47–57)
10. **Genetic Engineering**
   Jacob and the Spotted Sheep (VaYetze, Genesis 30:37–43)
11. **The Detective Story**
   The Unsolved Murder (Shof'tim, Deuteronomy 21:1–9)

12. Management Consultant
   Jethro (Yithro, Exodus 18:13–27)
13. Homesteaders
   Abraham and Nephew Lot Apportion the Land (Lekh Lekha, Genesis 13:7–18)
14. Real Estate Transaction
   Abraham Buying Land (Chayay Sarah, Genesis 23:1–20)
15. Sociology
   Israelites' Refusal to Assimilate in Egypt (Shemoth, Exodus 1–14)
16. Drama
   Korach's Rebellion (Korach, Numbers 16:1–35)
   Joseph and His Dreams (VaYeshev, Genesis 37:5–36; MiKetz, Genesis 41:1–57)
   The Binding of Isaac (VaYera, Genesis 22:1–19)
17. Hands On: Constructions Large and Small
   Noah and the Animals (Noah, Genesis 7:1–4)
   The Dietary Laws and Forbidden Animals (Shemini, Leviticus 11:1–31; Re'eh, Deuteronomy 14:4–21)
   The Twelve Tribes (VaYechi, Genesis 49:1–33)
   The Tabernacle (VaYakhel, Exodus 37:1–9)
   The Menorah (Terumah, Exodus 25:31–40)
   The Enclosure (VaYakhel, Exodus 38:9–17)

1. Editorial

In our contemporary society an event is validated when reported in the newspapers. Therefore, we imagine how the first story of mankind might have been treated.

When to Use. The editorial approach is used when the text provides a factual basis for making a judgment approving or disapproving specific conduct.

Setup. Constitute the editorial board at a newspaper. Decide what your collective view is on a particular controversial event and express it orally at the dinner table.

Background Facts. Adam and Eve are expelled from the Garden of Eden for disobeying God's command not to eat of the Tree of Knowledge. (Bereshith, Genesis 2:15–3:20)

Issue. Are there some acts that cannot be forgiven?

Playing the Game. Decide on an editorial point of view.

ADAM AND EVE AND THEIR JUST DESSERTS

Adam, the first man, was expelled today from the Garden
of Eden for disobeying an explicit command not to eat
from the Tree of Knowledge. After eating from the Tree,
Adam sought to hide and then placed blame for his actions
on Eve, the first woman. She blamed the serpent. Both
persons were ordered expelled from the Garden of Eden.
Ignoring a divine command deserves the strongest
condemnation. Moreover, Adam and Eve compounded their
unfortunate behavior by refusing to accept responsibility
for their actions. Adam was initially told that "on the day
you eat from [the Tree of Knowledge], you will definitely die."
We think he was treated very fairly by only getting
expelled into the human mainstream.

ANOTHER CHANCE

We do not quarrel with the justification for the expulsion
of Adam and Eve from the Garden of Eden. They disobeyed
an explicit command and received stern punishment. We
do think that the punishment is for too long a period.
No doubt both Adam and Eve will learn that the struggle
for food and existence is exceedingly difficult. We are
certain that if they were returned to the Garden of Eden as
before, they would never deviate from any instructions.
In judging them, we must keep in mind that they had no
way of learning from the experience of ancestors as to what
might happen to them in these circumstances. We think
they deserve a second chance.

Ideas for Other Editorials. Consider the question of apportion-
ing blame between Adam and Eve as a topic for other editorials.
God's instruction to avoid the Tree of Knowledge was given to
Adam before the existence of Eve. She is aware of the command.
Eve accepts the serpent's assurance that eating from the tree will
result in her "being like God." After eating the forbidden fruit,
she goes to her husband and presents him with the fruit, and he
eats it.

2. The Courtroom Game

When to Use. A courtroom game is useful to explore the ques-
tionable conduct of a person. You need one side to develop the

accusations charging that the conduct was morally improper and the other side to present the facts and argue that the conduct was justified.

Setup. Establish a courtroom by assigning the role of judge, prosecutor, defense counsel, and witnesses, including accusers and defenders.

Background Facts.

Isaac had grown old and his eyesight was fading. He summoned his elder son Esau.

"My son."

"Yes."

"I am old and I have no idea when I will die. Now take your equipment, your dangler [sword] and bow, and go out in the field to trap me some game. Make it into a tasty dish, the way I like it, and bring it to me to eat. My soul will then bless you before I die."

Rebecca had been listening while Isaac was speaking to Esau, his son. Esau went out to the field to trap some game and bring it home.

Rebecca said to her son Jacob, "I just heard your father speaking to your brother Esau. He said, 'Bring me some game and prepare it into something tasty. I will eat it and bless you in God's presence before I die.' Now, my son, listen to me. Heed my instructions carefully. Go to the sheep and take two choice young kids. I will prepare them with a tasty recipe, just the way your father likes them. You must then bring it to your father, so that he will eat it and bless you before he dies."

"But my brother Esau is hairy," replied Jacob. "I am smooth-skinned. Suppose my father touches me. He will realize that I am an impostor! I will gain a curse rather than a blessing!"

"Let any curse be on me, my son," said the mother. "But listen to me. Go, bring me what I asked."

[Jacob] went and fetched what his mother had requested. She took [the kids] and prepared them, using the tasty recipe that [Jacob's] father liked best. Rebecca then took her older son Esau's best clothing, which she had in her keeping, and put them on her younger son Jacob. She [also] placed the young goats' skins on his arms and on the hairless parts of his neck.

Rebecca handed to her son Jacob the delicacy and the bread she had baked. He came to his father.

"Father."

"Yes. Who are you, my son?"

"It is I, Esau, your first-born," said Jacob. "I have done as you asked. Sit up, and eat the game I trapped, so that your soul will bless me." (Toledoth, Genesis 27:1–19)

Issue. Isaac bestows the blessing due to the first-born son on Jacob, the younger twin brother. Rebecca is accused of masterminding, persuading, and actively assisting her son Jacob to misrepresent himself to his father Isaac. The objective is to receive the blessing intended for the first-born son. Judge whether Rebecca's conduct was appropriate under the circumstances.

Playing the Game. A possible transcript of a court scene that never occurred:

Question (by the Prosecutor):	Rebecca, you were the mastermind behind the plot to steal the birthright from Esau.
Answer (by Rebecca):	I did what I thought was right in order to have the birthright of serving as forefather of the Jewish people pass to the son who had the better qualities.
Question:	Are you saying that you committed an act of deception in order to safeguard a higher value?
Answer:	Isaac was a blind man, but not only physically. He could not see or would not recognize that our two sons were not of equal moral stature. My oldest son, and it pains me as a mother to say it, was not morally fit to serve as the successor to his grandfather, Abraham, or his father, Isaac, who were fulfilling God's

promise as the founding fathers
of the Jewish people. Even
while these twins struggled
within my womb, I was told
that Jacob was the destined
one. When they were adults,
anyone could see that Jacob had
the moral qualities necessary
for this unique role.

Developing the Game. We are suggesting merely the beginning of a courtroom trial that you can expand with the introduction of additional witnesses. Each of your family members can take a different role in examining Rebecca's conduct and its consequences for the Jewish people.

Ideas for Other Courtroom Scenes. Obviously, the actions of Eve in succumbing to the temptation offered by the snake to eat of the Tree of Knowledge and then, in turn, ensnaring her husband, Adam, present vivid courtroom possibilities. Indeed, you can both make accusations against and defend Eve, Adam, and even the Serpent. (Bereshith, Genesis 2:15–3:20)

Great courtroom issues are present in the story of the golden calf. The Israelites grow very restless when Moses does not return quickly from Mount Sinai where he has gone to receive the Torah. They ask that Aaron help them construct the golden calf. He does not protest. He advises and participates in the enterprise. When Moses returns, Aaron must answer for his conduct. You can develop his justification through the courtroom technique. (Ki Thisa, Exodus 32:1–35)

3. The Game of the Highest Stakes: Between God and Man

When to Use. Games of the highest stakes are useful to explore the instances where God communicates directly with certain exceptional individuals under extraordinary circumstances. When this occurs, you will want to consider why God has chosen to communicate, how the communication occurs, that is, directly or through a dream, and what the result of the communication is. While God should not be personified in your presentations, a person may be assigned the responsibility of helping to explain the reasons in the Torah for the communication on the particular occasion and the judgment that God renders.

Setup. Assign one or more persons to make the arguments. Possibly, another person should serve as the mediator, whose role it is to keep the negotiations moving. Each side should define what it is trying to accomplish.

Background Facts. God advises Abraham that He intends to destroy the cities of Sodom and Gomorrah because of the wickedness of the inhabitants.

Issue. Is there justification for God's proposed destruction of the cities because the "outcry against Sodom is so great, and their sin is so very grave"? (VaYera, Genesis 18:20)

Playing the Game. Read aloud:

> [Abraham says,] "Will You actually wipe out the innocent together with the guilty? Suppose there are fifty innocent people in the city. Would You still destroy it, and not spare the place for the sake of the fifty good people inside it? It would be sacrilege even to ascribe such an act to You— to kill the innocent with the guilty, letting the righteous and wicked fare alike. It would be sacrilege to ascribe this to You! Shall the whole world's Judge not act justly?"

> God said, "If I find fifty innocent people in Sodom, I will spare the entire area for their sake."

> Abraham spoke up and said, "I have already said too much before my Lord! I am mere dust and ashes! But suppose that there are five missing from the fifty innocent? Will You destroy the entire city because of the five?"

> "I will not destroy it if I find forty-five there," replied God.

> [Abraham] persisted and said, "Suppose there are forty there?"

> "I will not act for the sake of the forty."

> "Let not my Lord be angry, but I [must] speak up. What if there are thirty there?"

> "I will not act if I find thirty there."

> "I have already spoken too much now before my Lord! But what if twenty are found there?"

"I will not destroy for the sake of the twenty."

"Let my Lord not become angry, but I will speak just once more. Suppose ten are found there?"

"I will not destroy for the sake of the ten."

When He finished speaking with Abraham, God left [him]. Abraham then returned home. (VaYera, Genesis 18:23–33)

Note: Sodom was destroyed, so apparently it did not have even ten righteous inhabitants.

Developing the Game. Place another person into your discussion. Have someone serve as an unrighteous Sodomite who argues that Sodom should be saved, advancing arguments that it is not much worse than other cities and that its people were hospitable in permitting Abraham's nephew Lot to dwell in their midsts. You could argue that inhospitality to strangers, which some commentators suggest was the principal reason for Sodom's destruction, is exaggerated. What else would you be able to say during negotiations in order to try to avoid the destruction of your city? A more effective approach is to represent that you will repent for your past misconduct and learn how to live more righteously in the future. Is this a convincing position in light of Sodom's record of corruption?

Ideas for Other Games of the Highest Stakes: Between God and Man. The golden calf was recommended for a courtroom scene treatment focused on Aaron's conduct. Another important aspect of the story is the communication between God and Moses, which occurs when God advises Moses, who is on Mount Sinai, that the Israelites are constructing the golden calf.

God declared to Moses,

"Go down, for the people whom you brought out of Egypt have become corrupt. They have been quick to leave the way that I ordered them to follow, and they have made themselves a cast-metal calf. They have bowed down and offered sacrifice to it, exclaiming, 'This, Israel, is your god, who brought you out of Egypt.' "

God then said to Moses, "I have observed the people, and they are an unbending group. Now do not try to stop Me when I unleash my wrath against them to destroy them. I will then make you into a great nation."

Moses began to plead before God his Lord. He said, "O
God, why unleash Your wrath against Your people, whom
you brought out of Egypt with great power and a show of
force? Why should Egypt be able to say that You took them
out with evil intentions to kill them in the hill country
and wipe them out from the face of the earth. Withdraw
Your display of anger, and refrain from doing evil to Your
people.

"Remember Your servants, Abraham, Isaac, and Jacob. You
swore to them by Your very essence, and declared that
You would make their descendants as numerous as
the stars of the sky, giving their descendants the land You
promised, so that they would be able to occupy it forever."

God refrained from doing the evil that He planned for His
people. (Ki Thisa, Exodus 32:7–14)

4. International Diplomacy

When to use. The techniques of international diplomacy are
useful to explore the relationships between two different political units such as tribes, kingdoms, and empires.

Setup. Assign participants to serve as the diplomats representing the Israelites and those representing the Edomites.

Background Facts. The Edomites are the descendants of Esau,
who many years earlier felt he was cheated of his birthright
through the actions of his twin brother, Jacob, forefather of the
Israelites.

Issue. The Israelites are instructed to negotiate permission to
cross the land of the Edomites en route from the Sinai to the land
of Canaan.

Playing the Game. Moses is involved in international negotiations when he leads the Israelites toward Canaan. He must seek
permission to cross the land of Edom. Moses first seeks to cross
through the royal road, but is denied permission. He then seeks
to go through the side roads and offers to pay for what his people
consume in the land. Again, he is denied. The Israelites must
then avoid Edom and take a longer route around Edom. Interest-
ingly, Moses does not have much bargaining power. God has ex-

pressly ruled out any use of force against these descendants of Esau, who are kindred of the Israelites. He must accept their rejections and bite his tongue.

The text records the entire negotiations:

> Moses sent envoys from Kadesh to the King of Edom [with the following message]: "This is what your brother Israel declares: You know about all the troubles that we have encountered. Our fathers migrated to Egypt and we lived in Egypt for a long time. The Egyptians mistreated both our fathers and us. When we cried out to God, He heard our voice and sent a representative to take us out of Egypt. We are now in Kadesh, a city at the edge of your territories. Please let us pass through your land. We will not go through any fields or vineyards, and we will not drink any water from your wells. Until we pass through your territories, we will travel along the King's Highway, not turning aside to the right or to the left."

> Edom's response was, "Do not pass through my [land], or I will greet you with the sword!"

> The Israelites said, "We will keep on the beaten path. If we or our cattle drink any of your water, we will pay the full price. It is of no concern. We only want to pass through on foot."

> "Do not come through!" was Edom's response. Edom came forth to confront [the Israelites] with a large number of people and a show of force. Edom thus refused to allow Israel to pass through its territories, and Israel had to go around [the area]. (Chukath, Numbers 20:14–21)

Developing the Game. Designate an adviser to the King of Edom who makes the argument as to why the Israelites should be permitted on the terms offered by Moses or on other terms that are advantageous to Edom and that Moses can accept. How far could Moses go in making the offer more attractive to the Edomites, or had he gone as far as was reasonable? For example, Edom could demand an alliance with Israel and a share of the spoils the Israelites might acquire once they attack the Canaanite tribes. As a negotiating technique see if you can find either any benefit or detriment to Edom for failing to reach an accord. An agreement is more likely to result when both sides see a benefit. An agreement may also occur if it is the only or best way to avoid the threat of terrible consequences. What is likely to happen if neither is present?

Ideas for Other Uses of International Diplomacy. As the Israelites cross the desert toward Canaan, they find that they do not
have permission to cross the land of other nations, and they engage in warfare.

The King of Arad attacks them, but is defeated by the Israelites with the help of God. (Chukath, Numbers 21:1–3) By the
time they encounter the Moabites, the Israelites have a formidable reputation as a military power, which affects how the other
nations act. Military prowess affects negotiations. To offset an
adversary's power a nation will seek allies. Here, Balak the king
of the Moabites enlists the assistance of Balam who is versed in
occult arts to weaken the Israelites. Balam proves to be an uncertain ally. To Balak's astonishment, Balam blesses the Israelites because God has intervened. (Balak, Numbers 22:2–24:25)
The interests of allies may coincide only temporarily but alliances are rarely permanent. Lord Palmerston noted that nations
do not have friends, they only have enduring interests. What negotiating position does Balak have with the Israelites, either with
the assistance of Balam or without it?

5. Intelligence Gathering

When to Use. Intelligence gathering is needed when a person is
going to make a decision based upon the quality and type of the
information provided.

Setup. Create a spy organization that will engage in gathering
and evaluating critical information about potential adversaries.

Background Facts. Moses sends ten men into the land of Canaan to report on the quality of the land and the strength of the
inhabitants.

Issue. How to evaluate the information?

Playing the Game.

(The Mission of the Spies)

> When Moses sent [the men] to explore the Canaanite
> territory, he said to them, "Head north to the Negev, and
> then continue north to the hill country. See what kind

of land it is. Are the people who live there strong or weak,
few or many? Is the inhabited area good or bad? Are the
cities where they live open or fortified? Is the soil rich or
weak? Does [the land] have trees or not? Make a
special effort to bring [back] some of the land's fruits."
(Sh'lach, Numbers 13:17–20)

(The Report of the Spies)

At the end of forty days they came back from exploring the
land. When they arrived, they went directly to Moses,
Aaron, and the entire Israelite community, [who were] in
the Paran Desert near Kadesh. They brought their report to
[Moses, Aaron,] and the entire community, and showed
them fruit from the land.

They gave the following report: "We came to the land
where you sent us, and it is indeed flowing with milk and
honey, as you can see from its fruit. However, the people
living in the land are aggressive, and the cities are large
and well fortified." (Sh'lach, Numbers 13:25–28)

Ten of the twelve spies give a report that disheartens the Israelites because these spies emphasize and elaborate on the formidable obstacles that will face the Israelites if they try to enter the
land. Two of the spies, Joshua and Caleb, contest this evaluation
and say that with God's assistance the Israelites will prevail over
their adversaries.

Developing the Game.   Use this event to show how information
is evaluated for the purpose of making decisions. First, the information given permits the drawing of some logical conclusions
about the land of Canaan. If the land has milk, then it obviously
has milk-bearing animals that can also be used as a source of
meat. Also, this suggests sufficient arable land to support the animal population.

After hearing this information about the land and inhabitants of Canaan, how should the Israelites act? Conflicting recommendations are made by the returning spies. Ten of the spies
do not believe that the Israelites are sufficiently strong to proceed. Two spies believe that the Israelites can conquer the Canaanites with God's help. Why do the spies give such differing
evaluations? The key difference between the two groups is their
attitude. If you know a person who generally confronts a problem in a negative manner, then most tasks become impossible.
Persons who are realistically positive see difficult tasks as chal-

lenges. The problem for the Israelites was how to evaluate the differing interpretations of the spies.

Ideas for Other Episodes of Intelligence Gathering. To undermine the Israelite population, Pharaoh orders the Hebrew midwives to kill surreptitiously all male infants at the moment of birth. "The midwives feared God, and did not do as the Egyptian king had ordered them. They allowed the infant boys to live. The king of Egypt summoned the midwives and demanded, 'Why did you do this? You let the infant boys live!'

" 'The Hebrew women are not like the Egyptians,' replied the midwives to Pharaoh. 'They know how to deliver. They can give birth before a midwife even gets to them.' " (Shemoth, Exodus 1:17–19) Pharaoh is attempting to determine why his intended destruction of the Israelites by the killing of their sons is not occurring.

6. The Media

When to Use. The media is used when an event involves conflicting forces and is unfolding publicly.

Setup. A typical television newscast has an anchorperson, an on-the-spot reporter, and commercials.

Background Facts. The Israelites are on a spit of land surrounded by water on three sides when they first see the approaching Egyptian chariots rushing across the desert. Pharaoh intends to re-enslave them. Overland escape is impossible. (BeShalach, Exodus 14:2–10)

Issue. How do the Israelites react? Is the recrimination against Moses justified, or, even if justified, does it help get the Israelites out of their predicament?

Playing the Game. The television anchorperson can describe the seemingly hopeless situation. A reporter with some of the tribes can conduct interviews and obtain a range of reactions. The Torah records that some Israelites vented anger against Moses for getting them into this predicament.

"Weren't there enough graves in Egypt? Why did you have

to bring us out here to die in the desert? How could you do
such a thing to us, bringing us out of Egypt? Didn't we
tell you in Egypt to leave us alone and let us work for the
Egyptians? It would have been better to be slaves in
Egypt than to die [here] in the desert!" (BeShalach, Exodus
14:11–12)

According to the commentaries, the tribes broke into four different points of view. One group of tribes argued that death by
drowning was better than returning to slavery. A second group
favored surrender and slavery rather than death. A third group
counseled physical resistance, while the fourth suggested psychological warfare, bluffing the Egyptians through "fierce war
cries."* Reports of the menacing approach of the Egyptians and on-
the-spot interviews of a representative of each of the groups will
depict the Israelite predicament.

Developing the Game. A television panel interview with Pharaoh as the guest can examine his motivation for refusing to
permit the Israelites to leave the land of Egypt, his eventual ca-
pitulation, and his change of mind in chasing them into the Red
Sea, where he suffered the loss of his armies by drowning.

From time to time, break the questioning with a commer-
cial advertisement, imagining what "products" might have been
available in ancient Egypt, like matzohs, chariots, or chocolate-
covered locusts. The Egyptians had the latter in abundance after
the ten plagues were visited upon them. The tenth plague visited on the Egyptians for Pharaoh's refusal to permit the departure of the Israelites was the death of the first-born sons of Egypt.
You can even imagine an aggressive newscaster sticking a mi-
crophone in Pharaoh's face and asking, "Well, Pharaoh, how do
you feel about the death of your first-born son?"

A better understanding of points of view could come from the
anchorperson interviewing Moses and Pharaoh simultaneously,
with each giving justification for his actions.

Ideas for Other Media Events. Present the television news story
of how just one of the ten plagues affected the Egyptians, the reactions of the people, Pharaoh, and his advisers. Also, interview
Israelites to show how they were affected by the plagues. (The
Second Plague: Frogs. VaEra Exodus 7:26–8:11)

---

*Yakov Culi, *The Torah Anthology: MeAm Loez.* Translated by Aryeh
Kaplan. New York: Maznaim, 1979, Vol. 5, p. 181.

The story of the departure from Egypt and the forty years of wandering in the desert form the bulk of the Torah along with a detailed recitation of the laws given to the Israelites by God. Many episodes with dramatic possibilities are present and include the departure of the Israelites from slavery in Egypt, showing the bedlam that must have surrounded the effort to move hundreds of thousands of persons abruptly. Page after page of the story has provided the basis for various dramatic presentations on the stage and in film. Surely the family discussion can start with an episode and follow with a discussion of its implications. (Bo, Exodus 11:1–13:16)

7. Reordering of Events

When to Use. Reordering of events is used when the text presents a succession of occurrences.

Setup. Each participant is to decide on an order of creation and give a reason for selecting a particular order.

Background Facts. A wit, while admiring the Rockefeller Estate at Pocantico Hills, observed, "This is the way God would have created the world, but He ran out of money." Look at the order of creation spelled out in Bereshith, Genesis (1:1–2:3).

Issue. Does the order of creation affect how we look at the world?

Playing the Game. Place the work of each day's creation on a separate card: night and day; the sky; dry land; vegetation; the sun, the moon, and the stars; swarms of living creatures; livestock, beasts; man (male and female). Reorder the six days of creation, but give a reason for doing so.

Developing the Game. The final act of creation was man and woman. "God said, 'Let [man] dominate the fish of the sea, the birds of the sky, the livestock animals, and all the earth—and every land animal that walks the earth.' " (Bereshith, Genesis 1:26) Create man and woman at an earlier stage in the sequence and see whether a different role for them must follow.

Ideas for Other Reordering of Events. Another sequence that permits reordering is that of the ten plagues against the Egyptians (VaEra-Bo, Exodus 7:14–11:8).

8. The Social Scientist Conducting an Exit Poll

Imagine you are an Israelite who has an opportunity to leave Egypt with Moses and are asked several questions. (Sh'moth, Exodus)

> You say that you are leaving Egypt in order to go from slavery to freedom. Would you still depart from Egypt with Moses if you could assuredly expect to experience one or more of the following:
>
> 1. No meat for forty years;
> 2. Periods of intense thirst;
> 3. Dying in the desert after taking an aimless route through it for forty years;
> 4. Intense periods of lack of confidence in the leadership, including the senior leader who abandons you for weeks at a time;
> 5. Internal struggle that breaks into physical conflict with the loss of lives;
> 6. Warfare with foreign enemies;
> 7. Experience of awesome supernatural forces?

9. Crisis Management

Imagine you are the ruler of Egypt and have just been told by a young prisoner named Joseph that your dream indicates that Egypt will have seven years of plentiful harvests followed by seven years of famine. How do you evaluate the accuracy of this crop forecast and what steps can you take to avert disaster? Relying on instinctive judgment, Pharaoh appoints Joseph to manage the food supply. How much food is set aside each year, and of what type? What about spoilage and transportation and storage problems? Should the cattle herds be reduced now to permit setting aside larger amounts of grain, which cattle would otherwise consume? What was Egypt's policy during the famine about selling food to countries or peoples who did not have the foresight of planning for the famine? (MiKetz, Genesis 41:47–57)

10. Genetic Engineering

Jacob wants to acquire some assets to provide for his ever expanding family, which eventually numbers twelve sons and at
least one daughter. He has already worked for fourteen years and
has acquired two wives, Leah and Rachel. Jacob now proposes to
work for Laban for another seven years. Payment is set in a
seemingly random manner. Jacob will receive all of the spotted
sheep that are born to the flock during the period of his steward-
ship. To reduce the odds and ensure a faithful reckoning, all of
the spotted sheep in the flock at the beginning of the seven-year
period are removed. Jacob beats the odds by using genetic engineering. A higher-than-normal proportion of spotted sheep are
born during this seven-year period. See how he does it. (VaYetze,
Genesis 30:37–43)

11. The Detective Story

"[This is what you must do] when a corpse is found fallen in the
field in the land that God your Lord is giving you to occupy, and
it is not known who the murderer is. Your elders and judges must
go out and measure the distance to the cities around the
corpse."(Shof'tim, Deuteronomy 21:1–2)

   Assign each of two or three participants to represent cities.
Spread them away from each other. Then arbitrarily place a
corpse in their midst. No one is permitted to move. Measure the
distance from the corpse to the closest city. The measurement
determines the city closest to the corpse. The Torah states that
the elders of that city must accept some responsibility for the
death.

12. Management Consultant/Career Counseling

Jethro goes to visit his son-in-law, Moses, who has just exited
from Egypt with the Israelites.

> The next day, Moses sat to judge the people. They stood
> around Moses from morning to evening. When Moses'
> father-in-law saw all that [Moses] was doing for the people,
> he said, "What are you doing to the people? Why are you
> sitting by yourself and letting all the people stand
> around you from morning until evening?"

> "The people come to me to seek God," replied Moses to
> his father-in-law. "Whenever they have a problem,
> they come to me. I judge between man and his neighbor,
> and I teach God's decrees and laws."

Moses' father-in-law said to him, "What you are doing is
not good. You are going to wear yourself out, along
with this nation that is with you. Your responsibility is too
great. You cannot do it alone.

"Now listen to me. I will give you advice, and God will be
with you. You must be God's representative for the
people and bring [their] concerns to God. Clarify the
decrees and laws for [the people]. Show them the path they
must take, and the things they must do.

"But you must [also] seek out from among all the people
capable, God-fearing men—men of truth, who hate
injustice. You must then appoint them over [the people] as
leaders of thousands, leaders of hundreds, leaders of
fifties, and leaders of tens.

"Let them administer justice for the people on a regular
basis. Of course, they will have to bring every major case
to you, but they can judge the minor cases by themselves.
They will then share the burden, making things easier
for you. If you agree to this, and God concurs, you will be
able to survive. This entire nation will then also be able to
attain its goal of peace."

Moses took his father-in-law's advice, and did all that he
said. He chose capable men from all Israel, and he
appointed them as administrators over the people, leaders
of thousands, leaders of hundreds, leaders of fifties, and
leaders of tens. They administered justice on a regular
basis, bringing the difficult cases to Moses, and judging the
simple cases by themselves.

Moses let his father-in-law depart, and he went away to his
homeland. (Yithro, Exodus 18:13–27)

13. Homesteaders

Friction developed between the herdsmen of Abram's* flocks and
those of Lot. The Canaanites and Perizites were then living in the
land.

Abram said to Lot, "Let's not have friction between me
and you, and between my herdsmen and yours. After all,
we're brothers. All the land is before you. Why not separate
from me? If you [go to] the left, I will go to the right; if to
the right, I will take the left."

Lot looked up and saw that the entire Jordan Plain, all the
way to Tzoar, had plenty of water. (This was before God

___
*Abram was Abraham's name before God changed it (Lekh Lekha, Genesis
17:5).

destroyed Sodom and Gomorrah.] It was like God's
own garden, like the land of Egypt. Lot chose for himself
the entire Jordan Plain. He headed eastward, and the
two separated. Abram lived in the land of Canaan, while
Lot dwelt in the cities of the Plain, having migrated as far
as Sodom. But the people of Sodom were very wicked,
and they sinned against God.

After Lot left him, God said to Abram, "Raise your eyes,
and from the place where you are now [standing], look
to the north, to the south, to the east, and to the west. For
all the land that you see, I will give to you and to your
offspring forever. I will make your offspring like the dust of
the earth; if a man will be able to count [all] the grains of
dust in the world, then your offspring also will be
countable. Rise, walk the land, through its length and
breadth, for I will give it [all] to you."

Abram moved on. He came and settled in the Plains of
Mamre, in Hebron, and there he built an altar to God.
(Lekh Lekha, Genesis 13:8–18)

14. Real Estate Transaction

Sarah had lived to be 127 years old. [These were] the years
of Sarah's life. Sarah died in Kiryath Arba, also known as
Hebron, in the land of Canaan. Abraham came to eulogize
Sarah and to weep for her.

Abraham rose from beside his dead, and he spoke to the
children of Heth. "I am an immigrant and a resident
among you," he said. "Sell me property for a burial place
with you so that I can bury my dead [and not have her
here] right in front of me."

The children of Heth replied to Abraham, saying to him,
"Listen to us, Sir. You are a prince of God in our midst.
Take our best burial site to bury your dead. No one among
us will deny you his burial site to bury your dead."

Abraham rose, and he bowed down to the local people, the
children of Heth. He spoke to them and said, "If you
really want to help me bury my dead and [put her out of]
my presence, listen to me, and speak up for me to Ephron,
son of Tzohar. Let him sell me the Makhpelah Cave,
which belongs to him, at the edge of his field. Let him sell
it to me in your presence for its full price, as a burial
property."

Ephron was then sitting among the children of Heth.
Ephron the Hittite replied to Abraham in the presence of

the children of Heth, so that all who came to the city gate could hear. "No, my lord," he said. "Listen to me. I have already given you the field. I have [also] given you the cave that is there. Here, in the presence of my countrymen, I have given it to you. Bury your dead."

Abraham bowed down before the local people. He spoke to Ephron so that all the local people could hear. "If you will only listen to me," he said. "I am giving you the money for the field. Take it from me, and I will bury my dead there."

Ephron replied to Abraham, saying to him, "My lord, listen to me. What's 400 silver shekels worth of land between you and me? Bury your dead."

Abraham understood what Ephron meant. He weighed out for Ephron the silver that had been mentioned in the presence of the children of Heth, 400 shekels in negotiable currency.

Ephron's field in Makhpelah adjoining Mamre thus became [Abraham's] uncontested property. [This included] the field, its cave, and every tree within its circumference. It was Abraham's purchase with all the children of Heth who came to the city gate as eyewitnesses. Abraham then buried his wife Sarah in the cave of Makhpelah Field, which adjoins Mamre (also known as Hebron), in the land of Canaan.

This is how the field and its cave became the uncontested property of Abraham as a burial site, purchased from the children of Heth. (Chayay Sarah, Genesis 23:1–20)

15. Sociology

The population growth of the Jews, their distinctive social ways, and their insistence on keeping their own names rather than becoming Egyptianized made the Israelites unable to assimilate in Egyptian social life. To amputate the entire Israelite population at one swoop would not serve Egyptian national interests for the Jews' labor was essential to the state. (Shemoth, Exodus 1–14)

16. Drama

Korach's Rebellion. Moses' leadership was continuously challenged. Among the most dramatic and perplexing was the one led by Korach, who came from the family of Levi, which was accorded special leadership responsibility among the Israelites. Korach went too far, and God intervened to provide an extraordinary ending. A free-form dramatic adaptation of the text will generate discussion about the conduct of each of the characters and their situation. This script may help organize your presentation but need not be used verbatim. The story will quickly lead into a discussion about the legitimacy of authority and the appropriateness of God's intervention.

Script (Korach, Numbers 16:1–35)

Narrator:	Korach, along with Dathan and Aviram, lead a rebellion against the leadership of Moses.
Korach:	Moses, why are you setting yourself above the rest of us? You have no right to do so.
Moses:	You want proof. Wait until tomorrow. God will then show everyone who He has appointed as leader.
Moses (instructs his subordinates):	Let Korach and his entire party take fire pans. Tomorrow place fire on them and offer incense on them. God will then show His will.
Moses (trying to reason with Korach):	Listen to what I have to say, you sons of Levi. Why are you not satisfied with what God has already done for you? God has selected you, Korach, from the rest of the sons of Levi to serve Him in a special way. Only you are to serve in God's Tabernacle. Now you want more privileges and are demanding the priesthood! You are actually rebelling against God himself because God selected Aaron and his descendants to serve as the High Priests.
Narrator:	Moses then summons Dathan and Aviram, who are also part of the rebellion.
Dathan and Aviram answer:	We will not come! Moses brought us out of Egypt, a land flowing with milk and honey—just to kill us in the desert! What right does he have to make himself our

leader? Moses did not fulfill his promises.
He did not bring us to a land flowing
with milk and honey. We are not fools.
Moses cannot pull something over our eyes
again. We will definitely not come!

Moses (becoming   Do not take the offering of Korach,
very angry)   Dathan, Aviram, or their followers. I have
prays to God: not abused my leadership. I never did them
                     any harm, and did not take a single thing
                     that belonged to them.

Moses (then   You and all your party will have to present
talks to Korach):   yourselves before God. You and your
                     party will be there tomorrow along with
                     Aaron. Each man shall take his fire pan
                     and place incense on it, and each one shall
                     then present it before God. There shall
                     thus be two hundred and fifty fire
                     pans besides the pans that you and Aaron
                     will have.

Narrator: The next day, each one does as directed.
                     Korach rallies his whole party to the
                     entrance of the Communion Tent. God's
                     glory becomes visible to the entire
                     community.

                     God speaks to Moses and Aaron telling
                     them to separate from this community
                     because the destruction will be
                     instantaneous.

                     Dathan and Aviram stand defiantly with
                     their wives and children.

Moses announces: This shall demonstrate to you that God
                     sent me to do all these deeds, and I did not
                     make up anything myself. Here is the
                     way you can judge whether God chose me
                     to lead the Israelites. If these men die
                     natural deaths then God did not send me.
                     But if God creates something entirely new,
                     making the earth open its mouth and
                     swallow them and all that is theirs, so that

	they descend to the depths alive, then it is these men who are provoking God.
Narrator:	Moses has hardly finished speaking when the ground under Dathan and Aviram splits, the earth opens its mouth and swallows them, their families, their property and all their supporters. They fall into the depths along with all that was theirs. The earth then covers them over, and they are lost to the community.
	Hearing their cries, all the Israelites around them scream that the earth will also swallow them up, and they begin to run away. Fire then comes down from God, and it consumes the two hundred and fifty men who are presenting the incense.

Rather than performing a skit, you may vary the family presentation with charades, another form of drama that stimulates excitement in learning. Have each participant dramatize one of the ten plagues while the others attempt to guess which one is depicted.

Variations on a Theme. A family using the thematic approach could devote several discussions to the presentation of the experience of Joseph with dreams. First, Joseph has dreams about how he would be the overlord of his brothers. His telling them about the dreams enrages them. Then, his ability to interpret dreams frees him from imprisonment and raises him to the second highest office in Egypt. (VaYeshev, Genesis 37:5–28; Miketz, Genesis 41:1–57)

Other themes suitable for dramatic presentation appear at various places in the Torah and include rebellion against authority; deception; the significance of being the first-born son, and the plight of barren women. These will require general familiarity with the text or a more intense research effort.

Dramatize the Difficult Topic. The binding of Isaac is one of the most complex and thought-provoking stories in the Torah. Sarah, in her old age, bears a son, Isaac. He is the only child of Abraham and Sarah. Years later, God tells Abraham to take his "favorite" son to Mount Moriah and sacrifice him as a "burnt offering." Abraham makes the preparations himself and takes Isaac on the journey, which lasts three days. As they approach the mountain, Isaac asks where the lamb for the sacrifice is and Abraham responds that "God will provide." Abraham builds the altar, ties Isaac to it, and is about to slay him when an angel of God intervenes, saying: "Lay not thy hand upon the lad." God then supplies a ram for sacrifice (VaYera, Genesis 22:1–19).

Discussion. Any activity related to the story should provide an opportunity to express the feelings it provokes of puzzlement that God should make such a request and bewilderment or curiosity that Abraham should set upon fulfilling the request without even an argument. Stories such as this are hard to address in the sense that they seem to portray God in a harsh light or the Patriarchs as primitives. The approach usually taken by adults is to consider each of these hard stories philosophically. With children this approach is confusing. They do not need answers to all of their questions. They just need to know that it is okay to have questions and feelings about what they have read. Therefore, "How do you feel about this story?" is high on the list of questions that may be asked. Drama may provide enough of an answer merely by permitting everyone to experience the plight of the characters and their predicament.

17. Hands On: Constructions Large and Small

You may need an additional idea or activity to use at the family Torah discussion. Construction of the actual physical objects will help stimulate the conversation. The discussion will then center around the objects created. The constructions should occur prior to coming to the discussion.

Noah and the Animals on the Ark

Use stickers or pictures cut from magazines to depict the clean animals and several of the unclean animals that Noah was commanded to take. He was instructed to take seven pairs of every clean animal and two pairs of the unclean animals. (Noah, Genesis 7:1–4)

Discuss the characteristics common to the clean animals and how abiding by these restrictions affects the lives of Jews. (Shemini, Leviticus 11:1–31; Re'eh, Deuteronomy 14:4–21)

The Twelve Tribes

Jacob had twelve sons. The sons were Reuben, Simeon, Levi, Judah, Dan, Naphtali, Gad, Asher, Issacher, Zebulun, Joseph, and Benjamin. Jacob also had at least one girl, Dinah, whose mother was Leah. These were the original "children of Israel," as Jacob was to call them later. The descendants of each of the sons was a tribe of Israel.

An Activity. Create flash cards with the name of each son of Israel on one side and the symbol accorded to the tribe bearing that name on the other. At first, try to identify the name just by looking at the symbol. Then, attempt to organize the names in the order of birth of each of the sons. Also group the sons with their mothers. The twelve sons had four mothers.

Both the Torah and commentaries ascribe significance to the choice of names. (VaYetze, Genesis 29:32– 30:24) At the end of his life, Jacob blesses each son. (VaYechi, Genesis 49:1– 33) The contents of the blessings are incorporated into the symbols of each tribe.

The family discussion can expand into the meaning of names in the Torah. Also, the Hebrew name of each of the participants in the family may be discussed. From what family ancestor were the names appropriated, what other sources were used for names, and what Torah association does the name have?

The Tabernacle

Background. The Israelites in the desert construct a Tabernacle to hold the Ten Commandments, which Moses has carried down from Mount Sinai. In fact, the Tabernacle contains two sets of the tablets. Moses broke the first set when he became angry upon learning of the golden calf upon his first descent from the mountain. (Ki Thisa, Exodus 32:19)

Instruction to Contractor: Build a model of Betzalel's construction of the Tabernacle.

Blueprint.

> Betzalel made the ark of acacia wood, 2½ cubits long, 1½ cubits wide, and 1½ cubits high. He covered it with a layer of pure gold on the inside and made a gold rim for it all

around. He cast four gold rings for its four corners,
two rings for one side, and two for the other.

He made carrying poles of acacia wood and covered them
with a layer of gold. He then placed the carrying poles
in the rings on the ark's sides, so that the ark could
be carried with them.

He made a pure gold cover, 2½ cubits long and 1½ cubits
wide. He made two golden cherubs, hammering them
out from the two ends of the cover. The cherubs
were made on both ends from the same piece of metal as
the cover itself, one cherub on one end, and one on the
other. The cherubs had their wings outstretched upward so
as to shield the ark cover with their wings. They faced
one another, with their faces [somewhat inclined
downward] toward the cover. (VaYakhel, Exodus 37:1–9)

The Menorah

Blueprint.

The menorah shall be formed by hammering it. Its stem,
and [decorative] cups, spheres, and flowers must be
hammered out of a [single piece of gold].

Six branches shall extend from its sides, three branches on
one side of the menorah, and three branches on the other
side.

There shall be three embossed cups, as well as a sphere and
a flower on each and every one of the branches. All six
branches extending from the menorah's [stem] must be the
same in this respect.

The [shaft of the] menorah shall have four embossed cups
along with its spheres and flowers. A sphere shall serve
as a base for each pair of branches extending from [the
shaft]. This shall be true for all six branches extending from
the [stem of] the menorah. The spheres and branches shall
be an integral part of [the menorah]. They shall all be
hammered out of a single piece of pure gold.

Make seven lamps on [the menorah]. Its lamps shall be lit
so that they shine [primarily] toward its center.

[The menorah's] wick tongs and ash scoops shall [also] be
made out of pure gold.

[The menorah], including all its parts, shall be made of a
talent of pure gold.

Carefully observe the pattern that you will be shown on

the mountain and make [the menorah] in that manner.
(Terumah, Exodus 25:31–40)

The plans for the Tabernacle are especially detailed. Other structures are also recorded in the Torah, such as The Tower of Babel and Noah's Ark. Imagine the naval engineering problem for the latter. The plan must provide space and separation for animals who are predatory one upon the other. Adequate provisions for the trip must outlast the forty days of rain as well as the period thereafter when the water subsides and dry land once again becomes habitable.

The Enclosure

Blueprint.

He made the enclosure [for the tabernacle]. On the south side, the twined linen hangings were 100 cubits long, held by 20 poles, with 20 copper bases and silver pole hooks and bands.

On the north side, it was also 100 cubits long, held by 20 poles, with 20 copper bases and silver pole hooks and bands. On the west side, the curtains were 50 cubits, held by 10 poles, with 10 bases and silver pole hooks and bands.

The east side was [also] 50 cubits [wide]. The hangings on one side [of the enclosure] were 15 cubits long, held by three poles with three bases. The same was true of the other side of the enclosure's entrance, so that the hangings there were [also] 15 cubits [wide], held by three poles with three bases.

All the enclosure's hangings were made of twined linen. The bases for the poles were made of copper, while the pole hooks and bands were made of silver. All the enclosure's poles [also] had silver caps, and the [poles themselves] were ringed with silver. (VaYakhel, Exodus 38:9–17)

Designing Your Own Game

Getting at a moral value in the Torah is made easier by using the vocabulary of a contemporary occupation or activity. Marry these with the facts provided by a Torah situation. With this combination you can design your own game.

THE
COMMENTATORS

IT IS MY PLEASURE
TO INTRODUCE YOU TO . . .

A Commentator Is an Excellent Conversationalist

Many of the best known commentators are not personally available to accept an invitation to your family Torah discussion. Rashi lived in eleventh-century France; Maimonides in twelfth-century Spain and Egypt; Nachmanides in thirteenth-century Spain; Yakov Culi in seventeenth-century Constantinople; Samson Raphael Hirsch in nineteenth-century Germany; twentieth-century commentators would include Aryeh Kaplan and Nehama Leibowitz of Israel.

A good commentator is an excellent guest, always ready to attend and take part in the conversation. The best commentators are generally those who have attended table discussions for centuries. An etiquette exists for preparing your family table for a guest commentator. Before the guest arrives decide on a portion of the Torah for the family conversation. If you have adopted a line-by-line regimen you already know the topic. With the week-by-week portion you have your general place in the Torah. Then you will read and select the subportion you intend to discuss.

Pick your most friendly commentator and listen to the advice offered. The commentator may say some things that you already know, or the commentator may give you a few new ideas, or the commentator may shock you with a comment that you think is absolutely outlandish. Although shocked, you are a well-mannered host or hostess and handle the situation with aplomb. Moreover, you enjoy having guests who are somewhat provocative, even in very unexpected ways. Besides, you have respect for the commentator.

If shocked, you ask a few more questions about justification for the statement. Sometimes the commentator, when pressed, will provide the answer for taking a seemingly irrational position. Others at your dinner table may explain why the commentator is making the statement. When you understand the reason your feelings are somewhat eased, even if you do not quite agree with all the commentator has said.

A third possibility is that no one has a ready explanation as to the commentator's reason for the statement. Nonetheless, you may brainstorm the statement in an attempt to understand the perspective of the commentator. Do not despair even if you do not reach agreement with the commentator. Commentators often do not agree, one with the other.

The uniting force behind the commentators is that each is expressing serious thoughts about the same Torah. Commentators, not surprisingly, have distinctive personalities and approaches. Some give closer evaluations to the importance of each word of the Torah and its grammatical form, while others, with the same respect for the words of the Torah, develop a broader philosophical analysis of the message of the Torah. To yet another commentator, the Torah is an opportunity to bring together all the many traditions that Jews have developed through the centuries and to show how each of these is rooted in the Torah itself.

Using Commentary Is Not Foreign to You.   When you engage in Torah discussion, you are developing your own commentary. For the moment you are not publishing yours, and the only persons benefiting from your thoughts are those at the immediate table. In time you may have a special insight on some portion of the Torah to share with others.

The most familiar forms of commentary in our general society are the remarks each of us makes about a movie, play, or book. A reviewer has the professional task of serving as commentator for the general public. We may read a review before or after we have personally experienced the event. If before, then the reviewer's column gives us an idea about the plot, the characters, and the skill of the presentation. We may scan a review without any intention of reading the book or taking part in the event but only to get summary information of its main ideas.

We also read reviews after attending the presentation. Does someone else share or disagree with our general impressions? The reviewer also has the ability to draw broad lessons from the event, which the untrained viewer may not readily perceive. Once we read the reviewer's interpretation of a book or play's symbolism or allegorical meaning we say with recognition, "That's a very interesting point. I know exactly what the reviewer is saying." Or we may ask, "How in the world did the reviewer see that complex metaphorical meaning in such a simple and enjoyable story?"

Torah commentary may be used in ways similar to those of a review, but the Torah commentator starts with a different premise. The Torah commentator's intent is to explain what the Torah is saying, while a reviewer will often candidly admit to expressing a personal point of view.

For family Torah discussion, the commentary provides the springboard both to raise your conversational possibilities and to keep the conversation aloft. You read the Torah text and glance at the commentary on the same portion. Three or four main ideas will emerge, which can serve as the basis for the discussion. A few of these ideas will help the family discussion, either for straight conversation or through one of the games we have described. Moreover, the commentator may also provide an additional story to illustrate a point. You may have another drama for your family acting group that helps understand a point of Torah. If you read a second commentary, the discussion possibilities will expand. Each may have a slightly or wholly different view on the significance of a point within the Torah.

A Critical Distinction: Values Commentary and Those That Provide Data.
Commentaries discuss questions about the acts of individuals, groups, and God's role in the history of nations and individuals. A distinction is necessary here between the values-approach commentary we are suggesting you use for the family Torah discussion, and the great range of books that describe the life of the individuals and societies mentioned in the Torah. The books that seek to re-create how life was lived in antiquity we call "the data approach." Archaeology, paleography (ancient writing), and the carbon dating of fossil bones provide much fascinating data. Serious and gifted minds have developed methods for gathering and analyzing data and are continuously expanding what we know about that human society.

The data approach does not focus on the right or wrong of particular conduct. The data approach does not usually advance a discussion that is struggling with values. The right or wrong of particular conduct is not generally helped by knowing how the people maintained a water supply. Also, when we learn some data, it is extremely difficult to add anything personal because we generally do not have sufficient information either to challenge it or to add anything of significance. If a scholar informs us that a pottery shard found at a particular site is dated by archaeologists as from the Late Bronze Age and indicates that Canaan and Egypt traded, what can we add? Not much, unless we have other data about trade patterns of the period. When we have a discussion about an episode in the Torah with a values commentary, we are talking about the quality of the acts of people, how and why they behaved, and how our lives may be affected by learning from the examples of their lives.

Data can add to a values discussion. If we learn that in a particular time an extended famine was taking place in the land as a result of a change in weather patterns, then we may have a better understanding of why people were behaving in a particular way.

The difference between a "data" and "values" discussion is illustrated even in as unlikely a discussion as one dealing with whales, polar bears, or tigers. A "data" discussion would focus on information about the animal's blood pressure, activity, keenness of vision, speed, and sources of food supply. A "values" discussion would consider whether we have a responsibility to preserve these or any animal species from extinction.

A Torah commentary on animals would address questions about the relationship of humans and other creatures of this planet, not their vital statistics, habitat, or mating habits. The discussion might start with the following passage:

> Be fertile and become many, fill the land and conquer it.
> Dominate the fish of the sea, the birds of the sky, and
> every beast that walks the land. (Bereshith, Genesis 1:28)

A discussion could then follow on childbearing, population growth, man's relationship with nature and the animal kingdom, and the meaning of man's having dominion over the animal kingdom.

The Egyptian pursuit of the fleeing Israelites is a commonly retold episode every Passover. An archaeologist might describe the location of the sea, which parted and permitted the Israelites to cross on dry land. A climatologist might describe how natural forces, a strong wind, can pile up the waters of a shallow swamp and open a path. An historian might discuss the well-traveled trade routes available to the Israelites on their journey from Egypt to Canaan and the types of commerce that existed between the two areas. A literary analyst might suggest the dramatic powers or shortcomings of the scenes where Pharaoh permits the Israelites to leave Egypt, changes his mind, and gives vigorous chase, with the resulting destruction of his army. A student of word origins will discuss the term "Yam Suf," to show that what is commonly known as the "Red Sea" is really properly translated as the "Sea of Reeds" (BeShalach, Exodus 14).

A sustained family discussion is not likely to develop from these texts. No one at your family table discussion can add to or challenge the data. If a fact is questioned, we stop, possibly to research the answer and lose momentum or, more likely, to drop the topic. The opportunity for family conversation will quickly wither. The process will end before it begins.

The "values" commentary does not build on this type of data. A "values" commentator will raise an entirely different set of discussable issues. The only facts you need are those of the story to be discussed. Try another aspect of the Israelites march out of Egypt, when they were pursued and cornered on a peninsula. The Egyptians controlled the only land exit.

The commentators interpolate into the text the extraordinary circumstances. According to one line of commentary, the tribes hesitated when told to march into the sea, which had not yet parted. They demonstrated an understandable skepticism. One man, Nachson ben Aminadav, according to the commentators, leapt into the sea. The other tribes followed his leadership; they went into the water up to their nostrils and continued without fear, as God had instructed. At that moment, and only then, the Sea parted.*

Why were the other Israelites holding back from jumping into the Sea until Nachson acted? They had all experienced the ten plagues against Egypt, which finally convinced the mighty Pharaoh to permit the Israelites to depart. Was their conviction of God's ability to perform miracles undermined by the fact that God had permitted Pharaoh to chase the Israelites to the water's edge with the possibility of doom facing them all?

Was Nacshon the one who took a brave but foolish step because he did not calculate the risks properly? Is he properly regarded as a man of faith? Is he commended for doing the right thing in retrospect even though we do not know his reasons at the moment of his leap into the waters? We do not know whether he could swim. If he could not, then his act of leaping into the waters is all the more significant. If he could swim, then perhaps his act is diminished because his life was not placed at greater risk by the leap.

The other Israelites are more typical of people in general. Is the man of faith a touch misled or crazed? Is what he is doing

---

*Yakov Culi, *The Torah Anthology: MeAm Loez.* Vol. 5, pp. 196–201.

commendable? Do we now describe a man of faith as a person who is willing to act on inspiration or a visionary who sees beyond that of the average person? Were the other Israelites who followed Nachson acting in destructive group hysteria?

The line we draw on the distinction between values and data may be sharper than your actual experience. Data can add to our understanding of how and why certain personalities reacted in a particular manner. Knowing about the web of intrigue among the nations of the region can explain why a particular attack occurred or why an alliance was created. Nevertheless, keep this distinction between data and values firmly in mind as you choose the commentators you will invite for your family Torah discussion.

Choosing from Among the Value-Oriented Commentaries

Exotic origins add interest to commonplace items. An item handcrafted in a remote valley of Peru or on a lonely Pacific island is inherently more desirable than a similar one made by a neighbor.

By this measure, Yaakov Culi's *Meam Loez* should rivet our attention. His is among the most usable of Torah commentaries for family discussion. Written in Ladino 300 years ago in Constantinople, Culi's purpose was to create a work that would serve to educate millions of Sephardic Jews. Ladino is a form of the Spanish language. The Jews of medieval Spain developed a separate language, which they maintained when their Sephardic communities were re-established elsewhere after the expulsion of Jews from Spain in 1492. Communities were established in Turkey, Greece, on Carribbean islands, and in early colonial America. Even now, Sephardic groups, including some in present-day Israel, speak Ladino. By comparison, Yiddish is a German-based language used by Jews who lived in central and Eastern Europe. The only common characteristic is that each is written in Hebrew characters and has some Hebrew words in the basic vocabulary. Otherwise, no linguistic relationship exists.

Culi's objective was to provide a total Jewish education to a large Jewish population that was losing an understanding of its Judaism. They knew they were Jews, maintained some customs, but had little understanding of the Torah and the entire body of learning and practice it embodied. Culi wrote a line-by-line commentary on the Torah. He used this format for introducing considerable material concerning Jewish law, practices, and beliefs. Recently translated into English under the title *The Torah Anthology* and encompassing about twenty volumes, the work is well suited for Torah discussion, if you are prepared to recognize that some of what it says will not be in accord with modern nonreligious thinking. Some people are uncomfortable when reading texts on Judaism that show signs that Judaism may be, at times and by the standards of today, intolerant, legalistic, and discriminatory. Some of the stories may appear far-fetched or too fantastic.

This forewarning that Judaism does not always take the "enlightened" position is to disarm those who will find one or two examples to support an argument that little of the Torah is worth discussing because the commentaries are so dated. We suggest accepting the commentary on its terms and learning why a particular view developed.

Among the best of the contemporary commentators is Nehama Leibowitz, who established herself as an institution in Israel with weekly radio broadcasts on Torah commentary. A Hebrew University professor, she has synthesized and analyzed the classical commentaries and skillfully created her own distinctive style. Her readability and special insights have won her an army of admiring readers for the multivolume series on each of the books of the Torah, such as *Studies in the Book of Genesis*; *Studies in Shemot*; and so forth. The novice in Torah discussion will find some difficulties in using her works, but the beginning intermediate will use her commentaries with enthusiasm in preparing for the family table discussion.

The Torah: A Modern Commentary, published by the Union of American Hebrew Congregations (Reform Judaism), presents an approach that will be familiar to an individual with a general education. The commentary offers historical or literary explanations for passages that seem entirely unfamiliar to the contemporary reader. The commentary is based on different assumptions than those of all of the other commentaries listed, which evolve from the perspective of Traditional Judaism. A review of the section on VaYikra (Leviticus) in this Torah, when compared with the traditional commentaries will bring these differences into clear focus. On the other hand, a section in the Reform commentary, entitled "Gleanings," uses traditional sources.

The Art Scroll commentaries on the Torah is a detailed new commentary on the Torah, prepared in English from a strictly

Orthodox perspective. The running notations on each section are generally readable, but require some effort to understand. The perspective may be more difficult to accept for one who is not entirely in harmony with this viewpoint.

Samson Raphael Hirsch was a leading traditional rabbi in Germany in the early nineteenth century. His Pentateuch is an extensive commentary on the Torah of a somewhat philosophical nature and with broader themes. The use of the commentary by the reader who does not read Hebrew is somewhat undermined by the translator's use of Hebrew words throughout the English translation.

The traditional student of the Torah has always started with the commentary of the incomparable Rashi (Rabbi Shelomoh Yitschaki Solomon ben Isaac) of eleventh-century France. He has stimulated many of the commentators who followed, but his style is not quickly understood by a casual reader.

A one-volume translation of the Torah is an essential companion to any Torah conversation program. *The Living Torah* by Aryeh Kaplan is most readable and with its footnotes, pictures, and occasional maps will stimulate Torah conversation. Kaplan, trained as a physicist, was an extraordinary personality. He died recently while in his forties, having fathered ten children and written or translated 47 books in a twelve-year period. He was the translator of the commentary of Culi's *Meam Loez* (*The Torah Anthology*) from the Ladino into English.

Another single-volume Torah translation with limited commentary is *The Soncino Chumash.** The running commentary consists of brief observations by the important medieval commentators, such as Rashi, Ibn Ezra, and Nahmanides, Sforno, Kimche, and Gersonides. The presentations are terse and may not alone provide sufficient information for a discussion.

Possibly the most widely used version of the Torah translation in synagogues around the country is the *Hertz Pentateuch.*† We recommend not using these commentaries because they are too preachy and do not stimulate open-ended discussions. Written in the 1930s by the then chief rabbi of the British Empire, the commentaries try too hard to reconcile the Torah and the thinking of the time without really providing satisfactory answers.

---

*Reverend Dr. A. Cohen, ed., *The Soncino Chumash.* London: The Soncino Press.

†Dr. J.H. Hertz, ed., *The Pentateuch and Haftorahs.* London: The Soncino Press.

The Jewish Publication Society's *The Torah: The Five Books of Moses* (Philadelphia, 1962) is a relatively recent translation but its lack of commentary limits its use for family discussions.

The Quick-as-a-Flash Rating System for Torah Commentaries

We will on a scale of one to ten rate a large number of commentaries that you may wish to consider for your family Torah conversation. We have devised terms that benefit these discussions, and they are defined:

> *Entry Level Ease*—Ability to convey information to an individual who does not have substantial prior knowledge about the Torah.
>
> *Quick Study Value*—Ability to understand main points after five to ten minutes.
>
> *Conversation Sparker*—Generates new ideas that are immediately usable in family Torah discussion.
>
> *Paints Pictures*—Uses stories to illustrate issues raised by the Torah. These stories are readily adaptable for games and dramatic presentations.

Commentaries Especially Suited for a Line-by-Line Approach

1. *Title:* **The Torah Anthology (MeAm Loez).** Translated by Aryeh Kaplan. New York: Maznaim, 1979.

   Who: Yakov Culi

   Description of the Author: Rabbi in early eighteenth-century Constantinople. When Rabbi Culi died, the work was completed by several successors.

   Approach of the Author: Encyclopedic commentary, which relies on parables, midrash, and attempts to include vast information about the whole of Jewish law, custom, and belief.

   Entry Level Ease: 8

   Quick Study Value: 9

   Conversation Sparker: 9

   Paints Pictures: 9

2. *Title:* **Art Scroll Tanach Series.** New York: Mesorah Publications. Multiple volumes are being

prepared on all twenty-four books of Tanach, the Bible, in a monumental enterprise.

Who: Numerous contemporary Orthodox rabbis.

Description of the Author: Traditional rabbis in the United States.

Approach of the Author: The philosophical introductory comments at the beginning of each parshah provide a thought-provoking presentation of a coherent and very traditional point of view. The line-by-line presentation of the commentaries is not readily accessible to a person newly embarking on Torah discussion, for it requires familiarity with a terminology and method that develops only after study.

Entry Level Ease: 3

Quick Study Value: 3

Conversation Sparker: 6

Paints Pictures: 3

3. *Title:* **The Call of the Torah**. Translated by E.S. Maser. Jerusalem and New York: Feldheim, 1980.

Who: Rabbi Elie Munk

Description of the Author: Twentieth-century personality, who held rabbinic posts in Germany and in France.

Approach of the Author: Pays attention to the direct rational meaning of the text, though juxtaposed with the superrational. He cites the *Zohar,* the major work of Jewish mysticism.

Entry Level Ease: 5

Quick Study Value: 4

Conversation Sparker: 7

Paints Pictures: 5

Commentaries Especially Suited for the Weekly Portion Approach

4. *Title:* **Studies in the Torah.** 7 volumes. New York: World Zionist Organization Department for Torah Education and Culture in the Diaspora, 1958–

Who: Nehama Leibowitz

Description of the Author: A twentieth-century Israeli scholar and university professor.

Approach of the Author: The comparative and the analytical from a religious perspective.

Entry Level Ease: 7

Quick Study Value: 5

Conversation Sparker: 10

Paints Pictures: 8

5. *Title:* **The Living Torah**. New York: Maznaim, 1981.

Who: Aryeh Kaplan

Description of the Author: Late twentieth century from the United States, who published forty-seven books in twelve years and died at the age of forty-eight. Original professional involvement was as a physicist.

Approach of the Author: To present the traditional meaning of the Torah to any person capable of reading the English language. Adds to understanding through liberal use of maps, notations, detailed table of contents, index, and bibliography.

Entry Level Ease: 10

Quick Study Value: 10

Conversation Sparker: 10

Paints Pictures: 9

6. *Title:* **Meditations on the Torah**. Tel Aviv: Sinai Publishing, 1956.

Who: B. S. Jacobson

Description of the Author: Twentieth-century Israeli who gave discourses on the weekly Torah portion on Israeli radio.

Approach of the Author: Wrote book of series of lectures for Israeli broadcasting and to serve as introduction and initial guide to the Torah on each weekly portion.

Entry Level Ease: 7

Quick Study Value: 7

Conversation Sparker: 8

Paints Pictures: 7

7. *Title:* **The Torah: A Modern Commentary**. New York: UAHC, 1981.

Who: Rabbi W. Gunther Plaut; Rabbi Bernard J. Bamberger; Professor William W. Hallo

Description of the Authors: Twentieth-century American Reform rabbis and a professor from Yale University.

Approach of the Authors: The perspective of Reform Judaism, which on important assumptions and points differs markedly from those of traditional Judaism. The

"Gleanings" section presents some traditional rabbinic observations.

Entry Level Ease: 8

Quick Study Value: 8

Conversation Sparker: 8

Paints Pictures: 5

8. *Title:* **The Pentateuch**. Translated by Isaac Levy. Gateshead, England: Judaica Press, 1976.

Who: Rabbi Samson Raphael Hirsch

Description of the Author: A nineteenth-century traditional rabbi in Germany who was attempting to present an explanation of the Torah and Judaism that appealed to the contemporary mind but stayed within the boundaries of tradition.

Approach of the Author: Traditional and philosophical.

Entry Level Ease: 3

Quick Study Value: 2

Conversation Sparker: 6

Paints Pictures: 1

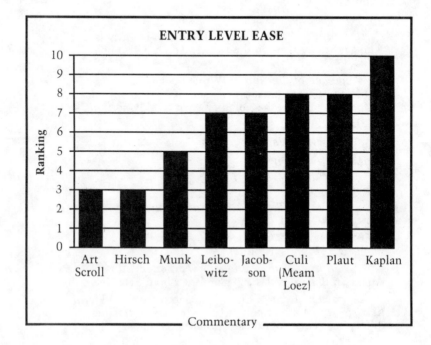

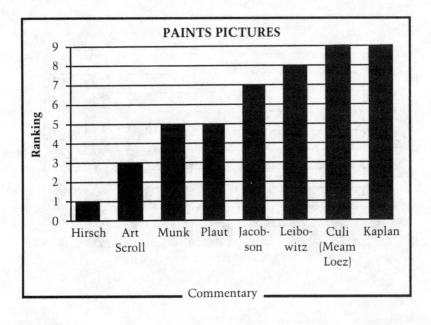

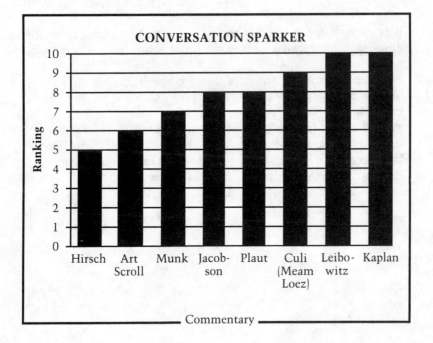

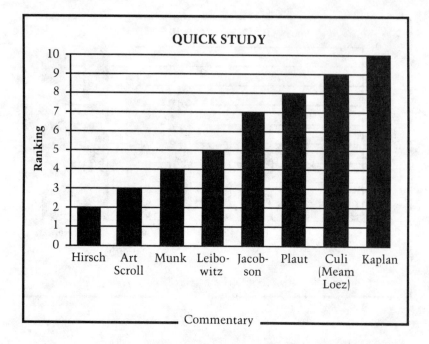

FOLLOWING DIFFERENT ROUTES
IN AN EXPLORATION

The different approaches of the commentators is apparent after
following each approach through a discussion of the same passage.

After leading the Israelites through the desert for forty years,
Moses is abruptly told that he has committed a sin and is barred
from going into the Promised Land. Was he barred because he
struck the rock from which water gushed forth or for some other
reason? How could a person of the stature and achievement of
Moses instantly lose the reward of his lifetime accomplishment?
Compare how several commentators discuss the nature of Moses'
sin and the punishment he suffered.

Yakov Culi, *The Torah Anthology*

Chukath   4   *[86]*

CHAPTER 4

20:12,13   וַיֹּאמֶר יְהֹוָה אֶל־מֹשֶׁה וְאֶל־אַהֲרֹן יַעַן לֹא־הֶאֱמַנְתֶּם בִּי לְהַקְדִּישֵׁנִי
לְעֵינֵי בְּנֵי יִשְׂרָאֵל לָכֵן לֹא תָבִיאוּ אֶת־הַקָּהָל הַזֶּה אֶל־הָאָרֶץ אֲשֶׁר־
נָתַתִּי לָהֶם: הֵמָּה מֵי מְרִיבָה אֲשֶׁר־רָבוּ בְנֵי־יִשְׂרָאֵל אֶת־יְהֹוָה וַיִּקָּדֵשׁ
בָּם:

God said to Moses and Aaron, ''You did not have enough faith in Me to sanctify Me in the presence of the Israelites! Therefore, you shall not bring this assembly to the land that I have given you.'' ❖ These are the Waters of Dispute (*Mey Meribhah*) where the Israelites disputed with God, and where He was [nevertheless] sanctified.

The Sin of Moses and Aaron

The Torah does not tell us explicitly wherein lay the sin of Moses and Aaron; it simply says, ''You did not have enough faith in Me to sanctify Me in the presence of the Israelites,'' without revealing how they had lacked faith in God. Our sages, however, have produced a number of insights concerning this matter.[1]

One source declares that Moses was guilty of four distinct transgressions. One, although God did not tell him to strike the rock, he did strike it; two, he failed to sanctify God's Name by drawing water from every rock to which the Israelites pointed; three, by declaring, ''Shall we produce water for you from this cliff?'' they made it seem as if it was not within God's power to draw water from any rock whatsoever; and fourth, God told them to ''speak to the cliff,'' that is, by studying a Torah portion near the rock to induce it to bring forth water, and they failed to do so.

It is these four failures which are indicated in what God said to Moses. ''You did not have enough faith''—God instructed them to resort to speech, and they struck the rock. ''You did not . . . sanctify Me''—they had done wrong in not bringing forth water from every rock. The sin incurred by saying, ''Shall we produce water for you from this cliff?'' also found indicated later in the Torah, in the Portion of *HaAzinu*, when

God says, "This is because you broke faith with Me in the midst of the Israelites at the Waters of Dispute" (Deuteronomy 32:51).

Finally, when, in the Portion of *Pinchas*, God says, "When the community disputed God in the Tzin Desert, you disobeyed My commandment [when you were] to sanctify Me before their eyes with the water—He refers to their fourth offense of not having expounded a portion of the Oral Law at the site of the rock.

[This fourth offense is alluded to in the words that chastised them for not fulfilling a commandment of God through speech. The obligation to study and transmit the Oral Law is such a commandment. In the present Portion, God says to them, "Speak to . . . (וְדִבַּרְתֶּם)"; and regarding the study and transmission of the Oral Law, the Torah says, "Teach them to your children and speak of them (וְדִבַּרְתָּ)" (Deuteronomy 6:7). Again in the Portion of *Pinchas*, the words, "You disobeyed My commandment (מְרִיתֶם פִּי), reflect the enjoinder pertaining to the Oral Law, to which applies, "God's Torah will then be in your mouth (בְּפִיךָ)" (Exodus 13:9).—Tr.][2]

There are other interpretations regarding the nature of their transgression. One says that when Moses contravened God's instructions and struck the rock, he lost the opportunity to teach the Israelites a great lesson. Had he instead addressed the rock and with a few words induced it to bring forth water, this would not only have exalted and sanctified the Name of Heaven, but the Israelites would have drawn the following moral for themselves: "If a rock, that has no capacity for speech and cannot hear and has no need for sustenance, fulfills the word of God, what of us who have seen such great wonders and for whom so many acts of beneficence have been performed?!" Thus would they have spoken, had Moses not smitten the rocks.[3]

A second interpretation states that Moses sinned by saying to the Israelites, "Listen now, you rebels!" This was an affront to the entire community; and for anyone who heaps insult upon the Israelite people as a whole, it is as if he is insulting God Himself.[4]

A third interpretation says that the needless anger that Moses directed against the Israelites led them to the conclusion that since such a great man as Moses could not be guilty of so demeaning an impulse as unjustified anger, it must be that God was angry at them for asking for water. That only made them doubt the justice of God's ways, since they felt themselves justified in asking for that without which they could not survive.[5]

A fourth view sees their transgression to stem from saying "Shall we produce water for you from this cliff?" instead of them saying, "Shall God produce water for you from this cliff?" After all, it was God who would be performing the miracle.[6]

A fifth interpretation says that they struck the rock twice. Had they struck it only once, their act would not have constituted a sin at all.[7]

According to another view, their sin lay in not having celebrated in song when water was produced.[8]

Others see their sin in the fact that they delayed fulfilling the demand of the Israelites until after inquiring of God. On their own they had the power to accomplish this, just as the prophet Elijah, in the time of King Ahab, controlled the dew and the rain and caused the fire to descend from heaven—and as Joshua on his own arrested the sun and the moon. Since this was a time of emergency, Moses could have achieved the same thing himself, and he should not have waited for God to tell him what to do. Had he done so, it would have greatly sanctified God's Name in the eyes of the Israelites. For it would have demonstrated that when a prophet commands a modification in nature, God brings it about.[9]

There are those commentators, however, who maintain that all the transgressions listed by our sages are not sufficiently severe to justify the decree that Moses and Aaron should die in the desert and not enter the land of Israel. After all, the breaking of the Tablets was a greater sin than any of these. Also, Moses' words, "Even if all the cattle and sheep were slaughtered, could there be enough for them? If all the fish in the sea were caught, would it be sufficient?" as was explained in the Portion of *BeHa'alothekha*, were a greater sin. Yet we do not find that on account of them Moses was condemned to die in the desert. It does not make sense, therefore, that for such a slight transgression, this harsh decree should have been issued against them.

Moreover, whatever God does is in consonance with the ruling of measure for measure as it is written, "For lovingkindness is Yours, when you render to every man according to his work" (Psalms 62:13). Here is revealed the pattern of divine providence whereby God perceives the deeds of each and every one, the good and the evil. But the decree pronounced against Moses and Aaron does not correspond to any of their aforementioned transgressions. What is more, Moses alone was guilty of those transgressions, not Aaron, who merely accompanied him. So why was Aaron punished?

We can only conclude that this judgment against Moses and Aaron was punishment for a terrible sin which each had committed earlier, but the punishment for which God did not reveal out of regard for them. It was at this time, when they committed the present slight transgression, that God exhibited His anger for that other sin.

This may be understood by the following analogy of a son who had sinned very gravely against his father. But out of consideration for the son, the father pretended not to notice. There came a time, however, when this same son committed a minor offense against his father, and the father beat him severely. Asked by the people why he punished his son for so slight an offense, he said to them, "It was not for the sin that I am striking him, but for that other grave offense that he had committed some time ago."

In the case of Aaron, his sin was related to the Golden Calf; and the sin of Moses was connected to the episode of the spies. Of course, Aaron was not personally guilty of worshiping the Calf, just as Moses was not guilty of the sin of the spies, but they were both guilty of causing the Israelites to sin.

Had Aaron refused to make the Calf and instead allowed himself to be killed, as Hur had done, the Israelites would not have committed the sin of worshiping the calf. For as we explained in the Portion of *Ki Thisa*, Aaron's motive was to put the Israelites off for a number of hours until Moses would reappear to spare them from becoming guilty of idol worship. The Israelites were nonetheless compelled by a desire for idolatrous worship and even with his commendable motive he was instrumental in bringing about the tragedy and in effect causing the death of thousands of Israelites who perished either by the sword or in the plague that followed. Accordingly, since it was because of him that so many people did not enter the land of Israel, it was decreed that he, too, should not enter the land of Israel.

Out of consideration for Aaron, however, God did not wish to make his punishment known at the same time that the others were punished. So He waited until they committed this minor transgression of striking the rock instead of speaking to it, punishing him for the sin that he had committed then.

As for Moses, his sin was this: When the Israelites expressed a desire to dispatch scouts, they merely said, "Send men ahead of us to explore the land. Let them bring back a report about the way ahead of us and the cities that we shall encounter" (Deuteronomy 1:22). This was in keeping with God's command to "Send out men for yourself to explore the Canaanite territory that I am about to give the Israelites" (Numbers 13:2); that is, merely to spy on the land. Moses, however, enjoined them regarding that which God had not commanded—to see what kind of country it was; whether the people in it were strong or weak, few or many; the quality of the populated areas; and if the cities were open or fortified (Ibid., 18,19).

True, his intentions were good, for he meant to provide the Israelites with advance knowledge about the giants, and men of might, and fortified cities that would nonetheless fall easily into their hands—all in accordance with the will and word of God, "Listen, Israel, today you [are preparing to] cross the Jordan. When you arrive, you will drive out the nations greater and more powerful than you, with great cities, fortified to the skies. They are a great nation, as tall as giants . . . But you must realize today that God, your God, is the One who shall cross before you. He is [like] a consuming fire, and He will subjugate [these nations] before you, rapidly driving them out and annihilating them, as God promised you" (Deuteronomy 9:1–3).

But the result was that the Israelites became alarmed by what the spies reported, leading to the tragic decree that that entire generation should perish in the desert. Since Moses was responsible for these consequences, he was condemned to die in the desert.

Out of consideration for him, however, God did not want to reveal his punishment at the same time that He pronounced judgment upon the others, and thus it was only now that He called him to account for that transgression.[11]

The Waters of Dispute

When Pharaoh decreed that every newborn boy was to be cast into the Nile, he specified this particular form of death because his astrologers had informed him that the savior of the Israelites was to be punished by water, which they mistook to mean that he was fated to die by drowning. In actual fact, however, he would be condemned to die for the sin of having struck the rock in an attempt to make it produce water. It is indicated in the verse saying, "These are the Waters of Dispute where the Israelites disputed with God, and where He showed His power against them." That is, the waters which the astrologers saw are "These . . . Waters of Dispute" on account of which Moses was punished; it was not as they had envisioned.[11]

CHAPTER 5

רביעי

20:14   וַיִּשְׁלַח מֹשֶׁה מַלְאָכִים מִקָּדֵשׁ אֶל־מֶלֶךְ אֱדוֹם כֹּה אָמַר אָחִיךָ יִשְׂרָאֵל אַתָּה יָדַעְתָּ אֵת כָּל־הַתְּלָאָה אֲשֶׁר מְצָאָתְנוּ:

Moses sent envoys from Kadesh to the King of Edom [with the following message]: "This is what your brother, Israel, declares: You know about all the troubles that we have encountered."

It is stressed here that Moses did not relax his efforts on behalf of the Israelites, notwithstanding that on account of them he was punished by being denied entry into the land of Israel. Although he would not himself come into the land, he was now designing a shorter route that would bring them into the land a little sooner.

When they found themselves in Kadesh, he sent envoys to the king of Edom requesting permission to use the much shorter road that passed through his land, thus avoiding a more circuitous path.

The message that he sent to the king of Edom said the following: "This is what your brother Israel declares. You know full well that we are both descended from Abraham, and that when God told Abraham that his children will be foreigners (Genesis 15:13), you too were included, and you should have suffered the same enslavement that we did. But your progenitor fled to escape this decree, as it is recorded, "Esau

Nehama Leibowitz, *Studies in the Torah*

Ḥukkat 2

MOSES' SIN

What was Moses' sin? The Torah refers to it on four different
occasions. Twice in our sidra:

וַיֹּאמֶר ה' אֶל מֹשֶׁה וְאֶל־אַהֲרֹן
יַעַן לֹא־הֶאֱמַנְתֶּם בִּי לְהַקְדִּישֵׁנִי לְעֵינֵי בְּנֵי יִשְׂרָאֵל
לָכֵן לֹא תָבִיאוּ אֶת־הַקָּהָל הַזֶּה אֶל הָאָרֶץ אֲשֶׁר־נָתַתִּי לָהֶם:
הֵמָּה מֵי מְרִיבָה אֲשֶׁר־רָבוּ בְנֵי־יִשְׂרָאֵל אֶת־ה' וַיִּקָּדֵשׁ בָּם:

And the Lord said unto Moses and Aaron,
Because ye believed not in Me, to sanctify Me in the eyes of
the children of Israel,
therefore ye shall not bring this assembly into the land which I
have given them.
These are the waters of Meribah, where the children of Israel
strove with the Lord, and He was sanctified in them.

(20, 12—13)

וַיֹּאמֶר ה' אֶל־מֹשֶׁה וְאֶל־אַהֲרֹן בְּהֹר הָהָר . . . יֵאָסֵף אַהֲרֹן אֶל־עַמָּיו
כִּי לֹא יָבֹא אֶל הָאָרֶץ אֲשֶׁר נָתַתִּי לִבְנֵי יִשְׂרָאֵל
עַל אֲשֶׁר־מְרִיתֶם אֶת־פִּי לְמֵי מְרִיבָה:

And the Lord spoke unto Moses and Aaron on mount Hor . . .
Aaron shall be gathered into his people;
for he shall not enter into the land which I have given unto the
children of Israel,
because ye rebelled against My word at the waters of Meribah.

(20, 23—24)

236

Again in a later sidra, *Pinḥas,* evidently in order to arouse Moses
to the need for a successor, after Aaron was no longer with him:

וַיֹּאמֶר ה׳ אֶל מֹשֶׁה
עֲלֵה אֶל־הַר הָעֲבָרִים הַזֶּה וּרְאֵה אֶת־הָאָרֶץ אֲשֶׁר נָתַתִּי לִבְנֵי יִשְׂרָאֵל:
וְרָאִיתָה אֹתָהּ וְנֶאֱסַפְתָּ אֶל־עַמֶּיךָ
גַּם אָתָּה כַּאֲשֶׁר נֶאֱסַף אַהֲרֹן אָחִיךָ:
כַּאֲשֶׁר מְרִיתֶם פִּי בְּמִדְבַּר־צִן בִּמְרִיבַת הָעֵדָה
לְהַקְדִּישֵׁנִי בַמַּיִם לְעֵינֵיהֶם

And the Lord said unto Moses,
Get thee up into this mountain of Abarim, and behold the land
which I have given unto the children of Israel.
And when thou hast seen it, thou also shalt be gathered unto
thy people
as Aaron thy brother was gathered;
because ye rebelled against My commandment in the
wilderness of Zin, in the strife of the congregation,
to sanctify Me at the waters before their eyes.

(27, 12—14)

And on the fourth occasion near the end of the Torah on the eve
of Moses' death in *Ha'azinu*:

וַיְדַבֵּר ה׳ אֶל מֹשֶׁה בְּעֶצֶם הַיּוֹם הַזֶּה לֵאמֹר:
עֲלֵה אֶל־הַר הָעֲבָרִים הַזֶּה הַר־נְבוֹ אֲשֶׁר בְּאֶרֶץ מוֹאָב אֲשֶׁר עַל־פְּנֵי יְרֵחוֹ
וּרְאֵה אֶת אֶרֶץ כְּנַעַן אֲשֶׁר אֲנִי נֹתֵן לִבְנֵי יִשְׂרָאֵל לַאֲחֻזָּה:
וּמֻת בָּהָר אֲשֶׁר אַתָּה עֹלֶה שָׁמָּה
וְהֵאָסֵף אֶל־עַמֶּיךָ
כַּאֲשֶׁר־מֵת אַהֲרֹן אָחִיךָ בְּהֹר הָהָר וַיֵּאָסֶף אֶל עַמָּיו:
עַל אֲשֶׁר מְעַלְתֶּם בִּי בְּתוֹךְ בְּנֵי יִשְׂרָאֵל
בְּמֵי־מְרִיבַת קָדֵשׁ מִדְבַּר־צִן
עַל אֲשֶׁר לֹא־קִדַּשְׁתֶּם אוֹתִי בְּתוֹךְ בְּנֵי יִשְׂרָאֵל:

237

Hukkat 2

**And the Lord spoke unto Moses that selfsame day, saying,
Get thee up into this mountain of Abarim, unto Mount Nebo,
which is in the land of Moab, that is over against Jericho;
and behold the land of Canaan, which I give unto the children
of Israel for a possession;
and die in the mount whither thou goest up
and be gathered unto thy people;
as Aaron thy brother died in mount Hor, and was gathered
unto his people.
Because ye trespassed against Me in the midst of the children
of Israel
at the waters of Meribah-Kadesh, in the wilderness of Zin;
because ye sanctified Me not in the midst of the children of
Israel.**

(Deuteronomy 32, 48—51)

The accusations levelled against Moses were grave indeed:

יַעַן לֹא־הֶאֱמַנְתֶּם בִּי לְהַקְדִּישֵׁנִי לְעֵינֵי בְּנֵי יִשְׂרָאֵל . . .

מְרִיתֶם אֶת־פִּי . . .

מְרִיתֶם פִּי . . . לְהַקְדִּישֵׁנִי . . . לְעֵינֵיהֶם

מְעַלְתֶּם בִּי . . .

לֹא קִדַּשְׁתֶּם אוֹתִי בְּתוֹךְ בְּנֵי יִשְׂרָאֵל.

**Because ye believed not in Me, to sanctify Me in the eyes of
the children of Israel,
ye rebelled against Me,
ye rebelled against My commandment ... to sanctify Me ...
at their eyes
ye trespassed against Me ...
ye sanctified Me not in the midst of the children of Israel.**

The place where the sin occurred is clearly located in our text —
at the waters of Meribath-Kadesh in the wilderness of Zin. The

238

Moses' sin

actual incident is recorded in our sidra 20, 2—11. But even a close study of the text fails to detect the exact nature of the sin. Isaac Arama devoted considerable attention to this problem in striving to find an answer. Recalling a Talmudic dictum he notes that we have everything,

> A table, meat and a knife before us but no mouth to eat with — the commandment of God is clearly outlined, the deed that was performed is not concealed from us and the subsequent wrath of God astonishes us, but no satisfactory explanation emerges.

We shall do what he advises, survey the numerous explanations advanced and note how they fit in with the texts we have quoted. Maimonides devoted a section of his *Shemonah Perakim* to this point, in illustration of his principle of the golden mean between the two extremes. Where man errs to one extreme he should go to the other in order to redress the balance. Maimonides then cites the texts bearing on Moses' sin at the waters of Meribah and concludes:

> His whole sin lay in erring on the side of anger and deviating from the mean of patience, when he used the expression "hear ye now ye rebels!" The Holy One blessed be He censured him for this, that a man of his stature should give vent to anger in front of the whole community of Israel, where anger was not called for. This behaviour in such a man constituted a profanation of the Name (*hillul ha-shem*), since he was the model of good conduct for all the people, who aspired to find their worldly and other-worldly happiness in emulating him. How would they regard anger in him, when as we have explained, that it is an evil springing from an evil side of one's character. The text "Ye have rebelled against My commandment" implies that Moses was not just addressing anyone, but an assembly the most ignorant housewife of which was reckoned as the prophet Ezekiel, as our Sages observed. Whatever he did or said would be subject to scrutiny. When they saw him thus in anger, they must certainly have concluded that he was not displaying personal animus or pique but, on the contrary, had not God been angry with them at their demand for water, Moses would not have been provoked. Yet we do not find that God was angry or showed disapproval when he told Moses to take the staff and assemble the people. We have thus in digressing

Hukkat 2

from our main topic succeeded in solving one of the obscurities of Scripture
— the nature of Moses' sin.

Maimonides refers to two sins — one a personal one of Moses in inclining to anger. But since this could not be read into the text "ye have rebelled against My commandment" he emphasises another offence, that of misleading the people by his display of anger with regard to the nature of the Deity. They would imagine that God was angry with them for demanding water and the All-Merciful was wrathful even when the occasion did not warrant it. They would imagine the Deity was a cruel forbidding God and not the Compassionate Father of all, hastening to quench the thirst of His people by commanding water from the flinty rock. In this sense Moses and Aaron had rebelled against God's commandment.

Naḥmanides takes Maimonides to task and refutes his arguments, citing the wording of the text.

> The Torah speaks of Moses not believing in God and nowhere mentions that Moses was angry or waxed wroth. Aaron was never guilty of anger — his whole life was one of peace-making and yet both Moses and Aaron were guilty of the same sin.

Naḥmanides concludes:

> We must admit that God was angry with His people for their disbelief "because ye despised the word of the Lord in your midst and wept before Him saying, Why did we leave Egypt?" Other texts refer directly to the Israelites striving with God "they are the waters of Meribah wherein the children of Israel strove with the Lord". What greater transgression could there be than this? Moses also remarked that the Lord was angry with him "for your sakes, saying, Thou also shalt not come there". How can Maimonides therefore maintain that God was not angry with them and it was Moses who gave the wrong impression?

Naḥmanides also rebuts the argument based on the fact that no allusion is made to God's anger in His command to Moses to speak to the rock and satisfy the people's thirst. He observes:

240

Moses' sin

Know that when men are in dire need of sustenance, even if they murmur and sin against Him, He the All-Merciful forgives iniquity and does not give vent to all His displeasure, does not refer to it but accedes to their request. The same happened on the first occasion when He answered calmly "Pass in front of the people . . . and smite the rock that water should go forth from it and the people may drink" (Ex. 17, 5), although the demand was accompanied by trials and strivings which were an example for all time.

Naḥmanides notes too that God did not show his anger with regard to the manna but sent it, in spite of His displeasure, merely informing them of their sin:

"I have heard the grumblings of the children of Israel". But when they grumbled for no cause whatever, then he poured out His anger on them. There was a difference between the Divine displeasure at complaints which had some basis and the anger at arbitrary grumblings as in the case of Korah and the spies.

Naḥmanides ends his attack on Maimonides' explanation with a triumphant quotation from the Psalms:

"And they angered Him at the waters of Meribah, and it went ill with Moses for their sakes" (Ps. 106, 32). The text thus includes this sin under the great trials with which they tried God in the wilderness.

Naḥmanides offers therefore another explanation citing Rabbenu Hananel.

Moses made the fatal mistake of saying, "Shall *we* bring you forth water", instead of saying "Shall *God* bring you forth water", as in all the other miracles where the authorship of God is always explicitly stressed (cf. Ex. 16, 8 "when the Lord giveth you meat in the evening to eat"). The people might have been misled into thinking that Moses and Aaron had extracted the water for them, by their own skill. Thus they failed to "sanctify Me in the midst of the children of Israel".

This explanation gains in plausibility when we recall that the children of Israel had, but a short while previously, left a land of

241

Hukkat 2

enchantments and sorcery and were very likely to attribute the production of water to Moses and Aaron's magical skill. Thus the two great leaders of Israel were liable to defeat the purpose of the whole Torah by their sin of omission. Their whole life was directed at propagating the idea of the omnipotence and providence of God and here was another golden opportunity of driving the lesson home. It may be argued, however that the people had been shown the hand of God on so many previous occasions that there was no reason to doubt that they would fail to discern the hand of God on this one. Naḥmanides anticipates this argument and endeavours to show that, on all other occasions, the hand of God was plainly visible. The last occasion on which they had been provided with water was accompanied by the appearance of the pillar of cloud standing over the rock (Ex. 17, 6). But here they saw nothing and by this the people were misled.

Naḥmanides adduces further proof for his explanation from the phrase: "Because ye trespassed against Me", since whoever benefits from holy things is called a trespasser. Moses and Aaron had benefited from a kind of misrepresentation, by not making clear that it was God who brought the water out of the rock. They arrogated to themselves something belonging to God.

How does Naḥmanides explain the other passages about "rebelled against Me", "did not believe Me?" —

> They violated the express command of God to "speak to the rock before their eyes" in order to sanctify Him publicly thereby. They rebelled in the sense of deviating from the command of God in not taking every step that was necessary to publicise the power of God. Or perhaps the phrase "because you did not believe Me" refers to the children of Israel.

Ibn Ezra takes a different view and sees the fault of Moses and Aaron not in their actions at the rock or in any deviation from the Divine instruction but in their undignified reaction to the people's grumblings and threatenings. He comments that "Moses and Aaron came before the assembly (verse 6) — "as fugitives" instead of

242

Moses' sin

sanctifying the name of God and showing initiative. There was no greater desecration of God's name than this. Joseph Albo reinforces this explanation, similarly taking issue with Maimonides and not accepting that the sin lay in the anger displayed by Moses, but rather in his display of lack of faith stressing the text, "because ye did not believe in Me".

A fundamental principle of the Torah and the root of faith emanating from the belief in His providence is that He subjugates nature to the will of the faithful, a thought which occurs in the Psalm to Moses (Ps. 91), the man of God that "He who dwelleth in the shelter of the Most High and sheltereth in the shadow of the Almighty" promises to deliver him from all snares, from all natural plagues, even to the extent of treading on the adder, viper, whelp and dragon. This is true of some righteous people, and how much more so of the prophets, for whose benefit miracles were constantly performed at their bidding! Elijah said: "As the Lord liveth surely there shall be no dew or rain these years except according to my word" (1 Kings 17, 1) . . . Moses himself said, "If like the common death of all men . . . but if the Lord will create a new thing . . . and it came to pass when he had finished speaking all these words that the ground beneath them did cleave asunder and the earth opened its mouth" (Num. 16, 29 ff.). Yet we do not find that God had previously given him command regarding this matter. Thus said Isaiah (44, 26) "He establisheth the word of His servant and the counsel of his messengers perfecteth".

Whoever doubts that the Lord will implement the word of the prophet casts doubts, as it were, on the Torah, especially where sanctification of the Lord is involved, when it is proper to publicise that nature is subjugated to the will of those who observe the Law. The failure of a prophet to perform miracles to save the nation is liable to make people doubt the truth of the text that the Lord establishes the words of His servants, especially when the prophet through whom the Torah was given, would not rely on the efficacy of his own faith to invoke a miracle, changing the order of nature . . . this is the implication of the text "because ye did not believe in Me . . ." had Moses and Aaron invoked a miracle to cleave the rock, the Lord would have undoubtedly established the word of his servant and been sanctified in the eyes of all the people. As it was, they appeared as fugitives at the entrance to the tent of meeting, as Ibn Ezra observes, as if they were at a loss what to do. This certainly profaned the name of God and caused a diminution of faith. Ye did not believe, in the sense of you had not sufficient faith to invoke a

Hukkat 2

change in the natural order. Aaron and Moses acted, as they did, out of a sense of their own unworthiness; they did not wish to usurp such authority. Nevertheless it was accounted an iniquity and a symptom of lack of faith because it gave rise to a profanation of the name of God ... You will find that Joshua, in similar circumstances did not wait for God to give him authority but relied on Him to do his will, and on his own initiative said, "sun stand still at Gibeon", and the Lord established his word. The Torah thus ascribes to Moses and Aaron the sin of insufficient faith, condemning them for not acting on their own initiative, without God.

Arama is thoroughly disgusted with this explanation and notes how what Rabbenu Hananel regards as trespass and rebellion is held by Albo to be desirable and creditable.

Moses never did anything except at the express bidding of God who never once disapproved of such obedience. Cf. "And the Lord said unto Moses, Behold I shall rain down on you bread from the heavens". The Almighty showed no disapproval of the fact that Moses had not produced, on his own initiative, bread and meat from heaven and earth. Afterwards at Rephidim the people asked for water — the same thing that happened in our context. Moses said: "Why do you strive with me and Moses cried unto the Lord saying, What wilt thou do unto this people? a little longer and they will stone me". By rights God should have been very angry at Moses' frenzied and impotent reaction. Yet God took no offence but said, "Pass before the people ... behold I stand before thee there on the rock and thou shalt smite the rock and water shall flow therefrom that the people may drink".

(Akedat Yizhak)

Arama likewise disposes of the argument that Moses and Aaron were perhaps prompted by a sense of their own unworthiness, by observing that it would have been the height of impertinence and folly for them to have desisted from sanctifying the name of God out of such considerations. Indeed, Moses and Aaron were perfectly correct in not anticipating a miracle from God. Arama is at pains to show that Moses had never acted on his own initiative not even in the case of Korah where the text explicitly notes that "it was not from my heart". Even the most trivial matter required a prior command of

244

Moses' sin

God, "The Lord shall command thee and thou shalt be able to stand up" (Ex. 18, 23). Joshua also had not ordered the sun to stand still, but had previously prayed to God for help, and it was only when he was answered, that he acted and spoke as he did. It distinctly says that the Lord hearkened to the voice of man (Joshua 10, 14) and not that the sun hearkened to the voice of man, as Albo would have it.

It is highly significant for us to observe how the approach of humility and discipline reflected in the *Akedat Yizhak* triumphs over the ecstatic miracle-working approach of Albo. We have to obey the commands and precepts of God and must certainly avoid any resort to miracles, to a revolution in nature. Even the greatest prophet has but to carry out the commands of His creator.

If Moses was neither guilty of arrogating to himself too much or not showing enough initiative wherein had he sinned? We are thus left in the position of the commentator (*Or Ha-hayyim*) who, having exhausted all the original explanations, decided to revert to the simplest one known to every child, that Moses struck the rock instead of speaking to it, as the Midrash explains:

> Four sins are referred to: "Ye did not believe" — wherein I did not tell you strike, yet you did strike; "Ye did not sanctify" to bring forth water from *any* rock they desired"; "ye trespassed" — that you said "Shall we bring forth from *this* rock"; "ye rebelled" — wherein I told you to speak to the rock, yet you violated my words.

Nahmanides who refuses to accept all the other explanations we have outlined likewise attacks this one. He regards the approach of the Midrash as purely homiletical and not at all supported by the plain sense of the text. Since God had explicitly bidden Moses to "take the staff" that itself implied that he should strike the rock. Had He insisted on him speaking to the rock, there would have been no need for the staff. Nahmanides cited Moses' carrying out the bidding of God in sending the plagues in Egypt, where he was ordered to take his staff and always for the purpose of striking with it. The text doesn't have to be so explicit but leaves it to be understood that he

Hukkat 2

was to strike the rock. In any case, the miracle gained nothing by consisting of speaking rather than striking.

Nahmanides also observes that the text itself records that Moses spoke in the hearing of the rock regarding the bringing forth of water from it. Moses' action could therefore not be termed trespass. He did speak to the rock. In spite of all this, the simple explanation is the most plausible and is accepted by one our later commentators Luzzatto:

> Moses our teacher committed one sin, but our commentators have heaped on him thirteen and more, each one of them having invented a fresh one . . . I have therefore hitherto refrained from going into this problem for fear I might attribute a new sin to Moses!

Luzzatto remarks that he had accepted for fifteen years the explanation that Moses and Aaron had acted like cowards and failed to sanctify the name of God by prompt and courageous action but in the end had to admit that it did not fit the text, which speaks of rebellion and not of cowardice. He therefore accepted the interpretation of Rashi that Moses should have spoken to the rock. Admittedly, as far as the rock was concerned, it was all one whether he addressed it or struck it. But to the ordinary folk it certainly seemed more miraculous if the rock gushed water at Moses' oral command rather than at his physical blow, and the name of God would have been accordingly sanctified to a greater extent. It but remains for us to refer to the ingenious interpretation advanced in *Ha-ketav Ve-hakabbalah* based on the text, "speak ye unto the rock *before their eyes"* (20, 8). ,

> It should really have said "their ears" since speech is apprehended by the organ of hearing. We must therefore conclude that not external sight is meant but rather insight — the mind's eye, just as the phrase "And their eyes were opened" in the case of Adam and Eve implied that they became conscious inwardly of a new state of affairs, and not that any physical blindness of theirs was suddenly cured. Moses and Aaron were bidden to act

Moses' sin

in a way calculated to impress the people with the omnipotence of God —
appeal to their insight, that they should be made aware of God's providence.
Rashi's comment, in the light of this becomes clearer: "Had you spoken to
the rock to bring forth water I would have been sanctified in the eyes of the
congregation who would have argued, If this rock which can neither speak
nor hear yet fulfils the word of the Omnipotent, how much more so we".

We have cited many different explanations of the problem of
Moses' sin. We can do no better than conclude with Maimonides'
own closing words to this subject:

Set what we have said, against what has already been said about it, and let
the truth have its way.

247

Aryeh Kaplan, *The Living Torah*

from the community. As long as the purification water has not been sprin- **19**
kled on him, he shall remain unclean.

²¹ This shall be to you a law for all times.

One who sprinkles the purification water [other than when it is done
for the purification ritual]* must immerse [both his body and] his clothing.
However, if he [merely] touches the purification water, [he must only
immerse his body]* and then be unclean until evening.

²² Anything that a person* unclean [by contact with the dead]* touches
shall become unclean. [Moreover] any person touching [him] shall be
unclean until evening.

[97. Miriam's Death; Lack of Water]

¹ In the first month,* the entire Israelite community came to the Tzin   **20**
Desert,* and the people stopped in Kadesh.* It was there that Miriam died*
and was buried.

² The people did not have any water, so they began demonstrating
against Moses and Aaron. ³ The people disputed with Moses. "We wish
that we had died together with our brothers before God!" they declared.
"Why did you bring God's congregation to this desert? So that we and our
livestock should die? ⁵ Why did you take us out of Egypt and bring us to
this terrible place? It is an area where there are no plants, figs, grapes or
pomegranates. [Now] there is not even any water to drink!"

⁶ Moses and Aaron moved away* from the demonstration to the Communion Tent entrance, and fell on their faces.* God's glory was revealed to
them.

19:21   **other than** ... (*Yoma* 14a; Rashi; *Yad, Parah Adumah* 15:1). This is true no matter how one lifts that
        amount of water.
—   **must only immerse** ... (*Ibid.*).
19:22   **person.** An Israelite.
—   **by contact with the dead** (Rashi).
20:1   **first month.** Nissan of the 40th year (Rashbam; Josephus, *Antiquities* 4:4:7), after the entire genera-
        tion of the Exodus had died (Rashi; Bachya; Abarbanel; but see Deuteronomy 2:16). There is no
        information about what happened during the 38 intervening years, other than the travels mentioned
        in 33:19-36 (Ibn Ezra).
—   **Tzin Desert.** To the south-west of the Dead Sea. Some translate it as "Desert of Palms" (*Adereth Eliahu*).
—   **Kadesh.** See 33:36. Also see Genesis 14:7; 16:14, 20:1. This is not to be confused with Kadesh Bar-
        nea, from which the spies were sent (Ramban; Bachya).
—   **Miriam died.** Some day that she died on 1 Nissan (*Seder Olam* 9; *Midrash HaGadol*; Josephus,
        Antiquities 4:4:6), while others say that she died on 10 Nissan (*Megillath Taanith* 13; *Targum
        Yonathan*; *Orach Chaim* 580:2). Some say that the Israelites arrived in Kadesh on 1 Nissan, and
        Miriam died on 10 Nissan (*Shalsheleth HaKabbalah*; *Seder HaDoroth*). It was about the same time
        that the message was sent to the king of Edom (*Seder Olam* 9). Josephus, however, has the encounter
        with Edom before Miriam's death (*Antiquities* 4:4:5).
20:6   **moved away** (Saadia; Ibn Ezra; Septuagint). Literally, "came."
—   **fell on their faces.** To pray (Ibn Ezra; Ralbag; Bachya), or to try to appease the demonstrators (Ral-
        bag). Some say that they fell on their faces to seek prophecy (Ibn Ezra; see Genesis 17:3, Ezekiel

[98. Water from the Rock]

20   ⁷ God spoke to Moses, saying, ⁸ "Take the staff,* and you and Aaron assemble the community. Speak to* the cliff* in their presence,* and it will give forth its water. You will thus bring forth water from the cliff, and allow the community and their livestock to drink."

⁹ Moses took the staff from before God* as he had been instructed. ¹⁰ Moses and Aaron then assembled the congregation before the cliff. "Listen now, you rebels!" shouted Moses. "Shall we produce water for you from this cliff?"

¹¹ With that, Moses raised his hand, and struck the cliff twice* with his staff. A huge amount of water gushed out, and the community and their animals were able to drink.

[99. Punishment of Moses and Aaron]

¹² God said to Moses and Aaron, "You did not have enough faith* in Me to sanctify Me* in the presence of the Israelites! Therefore, you shall not bring this assembly to the land that I have given you."

¹³ These are the Waters of Dispute (*Mey Meribhah*)* where the Israelites disputed with God, and where He was [nevertheless]* sanctified.*

1:28). This may have been the first time that God spoke to Moses after a 38 year hiatus (*Taanith* 30b; *Sifra* on Leviticus 1:1). See Deuteronomy 2:16.

20:8   **staff.** Some say that this was Aaron's staff, which was placed in the Holy of Holies (see 20:9, 17:25; Chizzkuni; *K'li Yekar*; *Zera Berakh* 2). According to others, it was Moses' staff, which had been kept in the Tabernacle (*Lekach Tov*; Abarbanel; cf. *Targum Yonathan*). This was the staff with God's name engraved on it (*Midrash Aggadah*). According to one opinion, God had told Moses to take his own staff, but Moses took Aaron's (*Tzafanath Paaneach*).

—   **Speak to.** Or, "Speak to [the Israelites] regarding. . ." (Ramban; Ralbag; Tur).

—   **cliff.** The hebrew word *sela* denotes a cliff or any other bedrock that protrudes from the ground, and not a loose rock on the surface. Some say that he was to speak to the nearest rock available (Ramban).

—   **in their presence** (see *HaKethav VeHaKabbalah*). Or, "to the first one they see" (Ramban).

20:9   **from before God.** See note on previous verse.

20:11 **twice.** Or, "a second time," referring to Exodus 17:6 (*HaKethav VeHaKabbalah; Mekhilta de Rashbi*).

20:12 **enough faith.** Or, "You did not work to make [the Israelites] have faith" (Saadia; Ralbag).

—   **sanctify Me.** See note on 20:13.

20:13 **Waters of Dispute . . .** See 20:24, Psalms 81:8, 95:8, 106:32. Also see 27:14, Deuteronomy 32:51; Ezekiel 47:19, 48:28. Cf. Exodus 17:7

—   **nevertheless** (Rashbam). Or, "sanctified through [Moses and Aaron]" (Ibn Ezra; cf. Leviticus 10:3). Or, "He was profaned" (*HaKethav VeHaKabbalah*). Or, "showed His power against them" (Saadia; cf. *Targum Yonathan*).

—   **sanctified.** *Kadesh* in Hebrew. Some say that it was for this reason that the place was named Kadesh (*BeMidbar Rabbah*; *Tanchuma* 11; Chizzkuni).

W. Gunther Plaut, *The Torah: A Modern Commentary*

The Second Murmuring

This is the second murmuring to take place at Meribah, the first being reported in Exod. 17:1–7, and in both instances water is miraculously provided from a rock. Bible critics have, therefore, suggested that we have here two versions of the same story. However, such a conclusion is highly speculative. It is equally likely that a return to the old resting place, which had seen a popular upheaval many years before, evoked memories and frustrations and led to a renewed complaint against the leaders who seemed to keep Israel forever in the desert. In fact, the focus here is less on the discontent of the people and more on the failure of leadership. It is in every sense a tragic tale which in its utter brevity raises serious questions about the sin of Moses and Aaron.

The Sin

Because of rebelliousness and lack of faith, the generation of the Exodus died in the wilderness. Now the same punishment is pronounced on its leaders, Moses and Aaron. However, the precise nature of the sin they committed is not clearly specified. The Torah says only that they did not trust God enough to affirm His sanctity (verse 12).

Most commentators see this lack of trust expressed in the manner by which Moses and Aaron executed God's demand to bring water to the thirsty people [5]. They were to have *ordered* the rock to yield water (verse 8), but Moses instead *struck* the rock twice with his rod, and the people were given water in this fashion. According to this explanation, the miracle was to have lain in the power of the word spoken to the inanimate stone in God's name. Instead, Moses

performed a physical act—not only once but twice—thereby revealing his lack of trust in the divine word[1] [7]. Other interpreters stress the apparent anger of the leaders. Moses says: "Listen, you rebels," thus addressing his own people in anger—but leadership and wrath do not go together [8]. Others note that Moses and Aaron say: "Shall *we* get water for you out of this rock?" thereby appearing to emphasize their own rather than God's role in the miracle[2] [10]. Still others take the Meribah incident to be merely the occasion for pronouncing judgment and consider the sins of Aaron and Moses worthy of the severe punishment to have been committed previously (Aaron's with the golden calf; Moses' with the spies)[3] [12].

None of these explanations (except the last, which however finds no warrant in the story itself) satisfies the question of how a minor transgression committed in frustration and justifiable anger could wipe out a lifetime of merit and service. Seen as an isolated incident, the punishment does not fit the crime. Neither striking the rock rather than speaking to it with confidence nor saying "we" instead of "God" is sufficient reason to keep Moses and Aaron from entering the Promised Land. However, the Torah does not question God's justice. Therefore some feel that the real sin of the brothers was edited out, in order to safeguard their reputation [13]. While that is a possibility, it cannot be proved. Moreover, the text *as it is* does contain the answer.

We must look at the story in the full context of the brothers' role as leaders of the people. On previous occasions when members of the generation of the Exodus had murmured, Moses had known how to

---

[1] The Koran, however, speaks of God asking Moses to strike the rock and, after he proceeds to do this, of twelve fountains opening up [6].

[2] Or that the sin lay in Moses likening his own powers to those of God [9].

[3] One midrash suggests that Moses' real sin lay in his having slain the taskmaster in Egypt [11].

deal with them. Now, at Meribah, it was the new generation, born or raised in freedom, who longed for an Egypt it had never seen or only dimly remembered and who still preferred the imagined comforts of the land of slavery to the trials of liberty.

To Moses and Aaron this regression must have come as a monstrous shock. It was as if their whole life's work, almost forty years of it, was wasted. In their younger days the two leaders would have recovered quickly and would have known how to meet the crisis, but somehow this time it was too much for them. In former days they had acted, now they were stunned into silence. They simply gave up and retreated to the sanctuary; they gave no reproof to the people and made no plea for assistance from God. They met the crisis with resignation and silence, two broken men seeking refuge at the door of the Tent [14].

Here lies the answer to the riddle. The faith that Moses and Aaron broke was their faith in the continuity of God's promise to an undeserving and rebellious people. In former days the brothers would have staunchly stood their ground, now the disillusionment of old age rendered them mute and passive. The Psalmist calls Moses a man of embittered spirit.[4] At Meribah of Kadesh, the rock of "strife and holiness," the ancient leadership was shattered. It broke because a new age demanded new vision, new faith, and undiminished capacity to sanctify the God of Israel to the people of Israel. If the Torah implies sin on the part of Moses and Aaron, it can only be the sin of failure: for leaders are always held responsible for the performance of those they lead. Both Moses and Aaron apparently considered the divine judg-

ment to be just and knew it to be irreversible. Aaron never raised his voice concerning it and Moses did it once and then ever so briefly (Deut. 3:23–25).[5]

Miriam is dead; soon Aaron will join her, and so will Moses before the end of that year. A new set of younger leaders is about to take their places and to guide the new generation of the people into the Promised Land.

Aaron the Man

What kind of person was the man Aaron who emerges from the biblical record? The Torah provides us with enough information so that we may attempt to picture him.

He held high office, the highest cultic position the fledgling community could offer. Yet even here he was, as in everything else, second to his younger brother Moses, and in a society that laid much store by the rights and privileges of the first-born this must at times have been a hard burden for Aaron to bear. It was almost always "Moses and Aaron" and rarely the other way around; it was Moses who transmitted the Torah to the people; it was Moses who invested Aaron with his duties, who led the people in war, and judged them in peace. Aaron would have been more than human if feelings of jealousy and frustration had not overcome him from time to time, and in a memorable—and for him psychologically disastrous—incident he joined his sister Miriam in an attempt to contest the supremacy of Moses (see Num. 12).

The fact is that Aaron did not possess his brother's stature. When he should have stood his ground firmly at the incident of the golden calf he failed, and no whitewashing by later generations can obliterate the clear

---

[4] Assuming that הִמְרוּ (himru) in Ps. 106:33 can be understood as if it were הֵמֵרוּ (hemeru), the verse would say: "They embittered his spirit and he spoke rashly."

[5] However, the Midrash lists many attempts by Moses to stay the divine judgment [15].

CELEBRATION

THE GIFT THAT LEADS TO A CELEBRATION

Many a touching story in literature describes hard-working and poor parents sacrificing to give their child a dreamed-about gift. The moral of these stories is usually the sacrifice of the parents rather than the child's excitement over receiving a valued possession. Their effort teaches the reader about the powerful force of a parent's love and sacrifice. The story loses its point if the parents are affluent.

A parent's involvement with a child in Torah discussion is a unique gift. The preparation and involvement in Torah discussion makes each parent an artisan, and as we know, handcrafted items are highly valued in an age of mass production. A parent who takes the time to shape a conversation on matters of importance is doing the work of an artist. The product will show personal brushstrokes even if they are slightly ragged at the edges. This personal creation will show affection and seriousness of purpose.

The result of family Torah discussion is not merely the conveying of information. If that is all that is desired, a prerecorded video cassette with an expert lecturing on the Torah could probably convey the facts better than a parent, but could not convey the emotional message that is evident in family discussion. The child observing the totality of the family Torah discussion process is learning important values, quite apart from the content of the discussion. An emotional experience arising from personal involvement molds character.

The child will eventually give a gift to the parent as the family Torah discussion becomes embedded within the family. Unpredictably, but inevitably, the child will make a reference to something learned at the table, or in an unguarded moment blurt out a nice word about the importance of this regular family event. This gift should give rise to a celebration.

Celebration or siyuum is the traditional Jewish way to mark the end of a period of study. The completion of a volume of learning from a traditional text is cause for celebration.

The same practice may be used to mark the end of a period of study in the Torah. One family celebrated the completion of its line-by-line regular Friday evening discussions of Bereshith (Genesis) by marking the occasion in several ways. First, each child was given an inscribed individual copy of the Torah. Second, a group of other families who shared the same practice of family Torah discussion were invited for a special event and were asked to present a charade depicting an incident in Genesis (Bereshith). Excitement developed as both parents and children shouted what incident was represented. Finally, parents and children offered individual experiences in family Torah discussions and shared ideas about unique approaches and the pluses and minuses of their particular method.

The timing of the celebration is not dependent on any fixed calendar. You may choose to call a celebration around the family table when you have completed a small amount of the text. The sharing of a delicacy at the meal can be announced as the marking of the event. Does anyone really need a major reason to have a small celebration?

We are at the end, your family is at the beginning—its creation!

A Year or Two
Down the Road

Our chapter "The Commentators" contains detailed recommendations for books that are immediately useful and necessary for preparing a family Torah discussion. Contemporary explorations focusing on the personalities in the Torah are contained in two short volumes that will serve as a complement to the main readings:

Wiesel, Elie (trans. by Marion Wiesel), *Messengers of God: Biblical Portraits and Legends* (Pocket Books, Simon & Schuster, New York, 1976).

Steinsaltz, Adin, (trans. by Y. Hanegbi and Y. Keshet), *Biblical Images: Men and Women of the Book* (Basic Books, Inc., New York, 1984).

Participation in family Torah study will also stimulate an interest in unexpected areas within the vast culture of the Jews. The annotated bibliographies in *The First Jewish Catalog* and *The Second Jewish Catalog* provide a spring board for further study. See Chapter 2, "Study," containing the section "Giving a Devar Torah" by Joel Rosenberg, pp. 238–252, in *The Second Jewish Catalog*, compiled and edited by M. Strassfeld and S. Strassfeld (The Jewish Publication Society of America, Philadelphia, 1976).

For an even broader bibliography see "Creating a Jewish Library," pp. 225–247, in *The First Jewish Catalog*, compiled and edited by R. Siegel, M. Strassfeld, and S. Strassfeld (The Jewish Publication Society of America, Philadelphia, 1973).

The Calendar
For Shabbat
Torah Readings

This calendar gives the date of the Torah portion cycle for each year. The cycle begins at Simchat Torah, which occurs in the fall. For ease of use, we follow the general calendar.

Explanatory notes:

When a festival or holiday occurs on Shabbat, a special Torah reading occurs that is not within the regular progression through the Torah.

If you are going to prepare for reading the Torah before your congregation, please verify the portion to be read with your rabbi.

	SHABBAT DATE	PORTION OF THE WEEK	CITATION
1986	January 4	Shemoth	Exodus 1:1–6:1
	January 11	VaEra	Exodus 6:2–9:35
	January 18	Bo	Exodus 10:1–13:16
	January 25	BeShalach	Exodus 13:17–17:16
	February 1	Yithro	Exodus 18:1–20:23
	February 8	Mishpatim	Exodus 21:1–24:18
	February 15	Terumah	Exodus 25:1–27:19
	February 22	Tetzaveh	Exodus 27:20–30:10
	March 1	Ki Thisa	Exodus 30:11–34:35
	March 8	VaYakhel	Exodus 35:1–38:20
	March 15	Pekudey	Exodus 38:21–40:38
	March 22	VaYikra	Leviticus 1:1–5:26
	March 29	Tzav	Leviticus 6:1–8:36
	April 5	Shemini	Leviticus 9:1–11:47
	April 12	Tazria	Leviticus 12:1–13:59
	April 19	Metzorah	Leviticus 14:1–15:33
	May 3	Acharey Moth	Leviticus 16:1–18:30
	May 10	Kedoshim	Leviticus 19:1–20:27
	May 17	Emor	Leviticus 21:1–24:23
	May 24	BeHar	Leviticus 25:1–26:2
	May 31	BeChuko-thai	Leviticus 26:3–27:34
	June 7	BeMidbar	Numbers 1:1–4:20
	June 21	Naso	Numbers 4:21–7:89
	June 28	BeHa'alothekha	Numbers 8:1–12:16
	July 5	Sh'lach	Numbers 13:1–15:41
	July 12	Korach	Numbers 16:1–18:32

SHABBAT DATE	PORTION OF THE WEEK	CITATION
July 19*	Chukath	Numbers 19:1– 22:1
July 19	Balak	Numbers 22:2– 25:9
July 26	Pinchas	Numbers 25:10– 30:1
August 2*	Mattoth	Numbers 30:2– 32:42
August 2	Massey	Numbers 33:1– 36:13
August 9	Devarim	Deuteronomy 1:1– 3:22
August 16	VeEthChanan	Deuteronomy 3:23– 7:11
August 23	Ekev	Deuteronomy 7:12– 11:25
August 30	Re'eh	Deuteronomy 11:26– 16:17
September 6	Shof'tim	Deuteronomy 16:18– 21:9
September 13	Ki Thetze	Deuteronomy 21:10– 25:18
September 20	Ki Thavo	Deuteronomy 26:1– 29:8
September 27*	Netzavim	Deuteronomy 29:9– 30:20
September 27	VaYelekh	Deuteronomy 31:1– 31:30
October 11	HaAzinu	Deuteronomy 32:1– 32:52
October 26†	VeZoth HaBerakhah	Deuteronomy 33:1– 34:12
November 1	Bereshith	Genesis 1:1– 6:8
November 8	Noah	Genesis 6:9– 11:32
November 15	Lekh Lekha	Genesis 12:1– 17:27
November 22	VaYera	Genesis 18:1– 22:24
November 29	Chayay Sarah	Genesis 23:1– 25:18
December 6	Toledoth	Genesis 25:19– 28:9
December 13	VaYetze	Genesis 28:10– 32:3
December 20	VaYishlach	Genesis 32:4– 36:43
December 26	VaYeshev	Genesis 37:1– 40:23

*Two Torah portions are combined on the same Shabbat.
† The final chapter of the Torah is read on Simchat Torah, which may occur other than on a Shabbat.

	SHABBAT DATE	PORTION OF THE WEEK	CITATION
1987	January 3	MiKetz	Genesis 41:1–44:17
	January 10	VaYigash	Genesis 44:18–47:27
	January 17	VaYechi	Genesis 47:28–50:26
	January 24	Shemoth	Exodus 1:1–6:1
	January 31	VaEra	Exodus 6:2–9:35
	February 7	Bo	Exodus 10:1–13:16
	February 14	BeShalach	Exodus 13:17–17:16
	February 21	Yithro	Exodus 18:1–20:23
	February 28	Mishpatim	Exodus 21:1–24:18
	March 7	Terumah	Exodus 25:1–27:19
	March 14	Tetzaveh	Exodus 27:20–30:10
	March 21	Ki Thisa	Exodus 30:11–34:35
	March 28*	VaYakhel	Exodus 35:1–38:20
	March 28	Pekudey	Exodus 38:21–40:38
	April 4	VaYikra	Leviticus 1:1–5:26
	April 11	Tzav	Leviticus 6:1–8:36
	April 25	Shemini	Leviticus 9:1–11:47
	May 2*	Tazria	Leviticus 12:1–13:59
	May 2	Metzorah	Leviticus 14:1–15:33
	May 9*	Acharey Moth	Leviticus 16:1–18:30
	May 9	Kedoshim	Leviticus 19:1–20:27
	May 16	Emor	Leviticus 21:1–24:23
	May 23*	BeHar	Leviticus 25:1–26:2
	May 23	BeChuko-thai	Leviticus 26:3–27:34
	May 30	BeMidbar	Numbers 1:1–4:20
	June 6	Naso	Numbers 4:21–7:89

*Two Torah portions are combined on the same Shabbat.

SHABBAT DATE	PORTION OF THE WEEK	CITATION
June 13	BeHa'alothekha	Numbers 8:1–12:16
June 20	Sh'lach	Numbers 13:1–15:41
June 27	Korach	Numbers 16:1–18:32
July 4	Chukath	Numbers 19:1–22:1
July 11	Balak	Numbers 22:2–25:9
July 18	Pinchas	Numbers 25:10–30:1
July 25*	Mattoth	Numbers 30:2–32:42
July 25	Massey	Numbers 33:1–36:13
August 1	Devarim	Deuteronomy 1:1–3:22
August 8	VeEthChanan	Deuteronomy 3:23–7:11
August 15	Ekev	Deuteronomy 7:12–11:25
August 22	Re'eh	Deuteronomy 11:26–16:17
August 29	Shof'tim	Deuteronomy 16:18–21:9
September 5	Ki Thetze	Deuteronomy 21:10–25:18
September 12	Ki Thavo	Deuteronomy 26:1–29:8
September 19*	Netzavim	Deuteronomy 29:9–30:20
September 19	VaYelekh	Deuteronomy 31:1–31:30
September 26	HaAzinu	Deuteronomy 32:1–32:52
October 16†	VeZoth HaBerakhah	Deuteronomy 33:1–34:12
October 17	Bereshith	Genesis 1:1–6:8
October 24	Noah	Genesis 6:9–11:32
October 31	Lekh Lekha	Genesis 12:1–17:27
November 7	VaYera	Genesis 18:1–22:24
November 14	Chayay Sarah	Genesis 23:1–25:18
November 21	Toledoth	Genesis 25:19–28:9

*Two Torah portions are combined on the same Shabbat.
†The final chapter of the Torah is read on Simchat Torah, which may occur other than on a Shabbat.

	SHABBAT DATE	PORTION OF THE WEEK	CITATION
	November 28	VaYetze	Genesis 28:10–32:3
	December 5	VaYishlach	Genesis 32:4–36:43
	December 12	VaYeshev	Genesis 37:1–40:23
	December 19	MiKetz	Genesis 41:1–44:17
	December 26	VaYigash	Genesis 44:18–47:27
1988	January 2	VaYechi	Genesis 47:28–50:26
	January 9	Shemoth	Exodus 1:1–6:1
	January 16	VaEra	Exodus 6:2–9:35
	January 23	Bo	Exodus 10:1–13:16
	January 30	BeShalach	Exodus 13:17–17:16
	February 6	Yithro	Exodus 18:1–20:23
	February 13	Mishpatim	Exodus 21:1–24:18
	February 20	Terumah	Exodus 25:1–27:19
	February 27	Tetzaveh	Exodus 27:20–30:10
	March 5	Ki Thisa	Exodus 30:11–34:35
	March 12*	VaYakhel	Exodus 35:1–38:20
	March 12	Pekudey	Exodus 38:21–40:38
	March 19	VaYikra	Leviticus 1:1–5:26
	March 26	Tzav	Leviticus 6:1–8:36
	April 16	Shemini	Leviticus 9:1–11:47
	April 23*	Tazria	Leviticus 12:1–13:59
	April 23	Metzorah	Leviticus 14:1–15:33
	April 30*	Acharey Moth	Leviticus 16:1–18:30
	April 30	Kedoshim	Leviticus 19:1–20:27
	May 7	Emor	Leviticus 21:1–24:23
	May 14*	BeHar	Leviticus 25:1–26:2

*Two Torah portions are combined on the same Shabbat.

	SHABBAT DATE	PORTION OF THE WEEK	CITATION
	May 14	BeChuko-thai	Leviticus 26:3–27:34
	May 21	BeMidbar	Numbers 1:1–4:20
	May 28	Naso	Numbers 4:21–7:89
	June 4	BeHa'alothekha	Numbers 8:1–12:16
	June 11	Sh'lach	Numbers 13:1–15:41
	June 18	Korach	Numbers 16:1–18:32
	June 25	Chukath	Numbers 19:1–22:1
	July 2	Balak	Numbers 22:2–25:9
	July 9	Pinchas	Numbers 25:10–30:1
	July 16*	Mattoth	Numbers 30:2–32:42
	July 16	Massey	Numbers 33:1–36:13
	July 23	Devarim	Deuteronomy 1:1–3:22
	July 30	VeEthChanan	Deuteronomy 3:23–7:11
	August 6	Ekev	Deuteronomy 7:12–11:25
	August 13	Re'eh	Deuteronomy 11:26–16:17
	August 20	Shof'tim	Deuteronomy 16:18–21:9
	August 27	Ki Thetze	Deuteronomy 21:10–25:18
	September 3	Ki Thavo	Deuteronomy 26:1–29:8
	September 10	Netzavim	Deuteronomy 29:9–30:20
	September 17	VaYelekh	Deuteronomy 31:1–31:30
	September 24	HaAzinu	Deuteronomy 32:1–32:52
	October 4†	VeZoth HaBerakhah	Deuteronomy 33:1–34:12
	October 8	Bereshith	Genesis 1:1–6:8
	October 15	Noah	Genesis 6:9–11:32
	October 22	Lekh Lekha	Genesis 12:1–17:27

*Two Torah portions are combined on the same Shabbat.
†The final chapter of the Torah is read on Simchat Torah, which may occur other than on a Shabbat.

	SHABBAT DATE	PORTION OF THE WEEK	CITATION
	October 29	VaYera	Genesis 18:1–22:24
	November 5	Chayay Sarah	Genesis 23:1–25:18
	November 12	Toledoth	Genesis 25:19–28:9
	November 19	VaYetze	Genesis 28:10–32:3
	November 26	VaYishlach	Genesis 32:4–36:43
	December 3	VaYeshev	Genesis 37:1–40:23
	December 10	MiKetz	Genesis 41:1–44:17
	December 17	VaYigash	Genesis 44:18–47:27
	December 24	VaYechi	Genesis 47:28–50:26
	December 31	Shemot	Exodus 1:1–6:1
1989	January 7	VaEra	Exodus 6:2–9:35
	January 14	Bo	Exodus 10:1–13:16
	January 21	BeShalach	Exodus 13:17–17:16
	January 28	Yithro	Exodus 18:1–20:23
	February 4	Mishpatim	Exodus 21:1–24:18
	February 11	Terumah	Exodus 25:1–27:19
	February 18	Tetzaveh	Exodus 27:20–30:10
	February 25	Ki Thisa	Exodus 30:11–34:35
	March 4	VaYakhel	Exodus 35:1–38:20
	March 11	Pekudey	Exodus 38:21–40:38
	March 18	VaYikra	Leviticus 1:1–5:26
	March 25	Tzav	Leviticus 6:1–8:36
	April 1	Shemini	Leviticus 9:1–11:47
	April 8	Tazria	Leviticus 12:1–13:59
	April 15	Metzorah	Leviticus 14:1–15:33
	April 29	Acharey Moth	Leviticus 16:1–18:30
	May 6	Kedoshim	Leviticus 19:1–20:27

SHABBAT DATE	PORTION OF THE WEEK	CITATION
May 13	Emor	Leviticus 21:1–24:23
May 20	BeHar	Leviticus 25:1–26:2
May 27	BeChuko-thai	Leviticus 26:3–27:34
June 3	BeMidbar	Numbers 1:1–4:20
June 17	Naso	Numbers 4:21–7:89
June 24	BeHa'alothekha	Numbers 8:1–12:16
July 1	Sh'lach	Numbers 13:1–15:41
July 8	Korach	Numbers 16:1–18:32
July 15*	Chukath	Numbers 19:1–22:1
July 15	Balak	Numbers 22:2–25:9
July 22	Pinchas	Numbers 25:10–30:1
July 29*	Mattoth	Numbers 30:2–32:42
July 29	Massey	Numbers 33:1–36:13
August 5	Devarim	Deuteronomy 1:1–3:22
August 12	VeEthChanan	Deuteronomy 3:23–7:11
August 19	Ekev	Deuteronomy 7:12–11:25
August 26	Re'eh	Deuteronomy 11:26–16:17
September 2	Shof'tim	Deuteronomy 16:18–21:9
September 9	Ki Thetze	Deuteronomy 21:10–25:18
September 16	Ki Thavo	Deuteronomy 26:1–29:8
September 23*	Netzavim	Deuteronomy 29:9–30:20
September 23	VaYelekh	Deuteronomy 31:1–31:30
October 7	HaAzinu	Deuteronomy 32:1–32:52
October 22†	VeZoth HaBerakhah	Deuteronomy 33:1–34:12
October 28	Bereshith	Genesis 1:1–6:8

*Two Torah portions are combined on the same Shabbat.

†The final chapter of the Torah is read on Simchat Torah, which may occur other than on a Shabbat.

	SHABBAT DATE	PORTION OF THE WEEK	CITATION
	November 4	Noah	Genesis 6:9–11:32
	November 11	Lekh Lekha	Genesis 12:1–17:27
	November 18	VaYera	Genesis 18:1–22:24
	November 25	Chayay Sarah	Genesis 23:1–25:18
	December 2	Toledoth	Genesis 25:19–28:9
	December 9	VaYetze	Genesis 28:10–32:3
	December 16	VaYishlach	Genesis 32:4–36:43
	December 23	VaYeshev	Genesis 37:1–40:23
	December 30	MiKetz	Genesis 41:1–44:17
1990	January 6	VaYigash	Genesis 44:18–47:27
	January 13	VaYechi	Genesis 47:28–50:26
	January 20	Shemoth	Exodus 1:1–6:1
	January 27	VaEra	Exodus 6:2–9:35
	February 3	Bo	Exodus 10:1–13:16
	February 10	BeShalach	Exodus 13:17–17:16
	February 17	Yithro	Exodus 18:1–20:23
	February 24	Mishpatim	Exodus 21:1–24:18
	March 3	Terumah	Exodus 25:1–27:19
	March 10	Tetzaveh	Exodus 27:20–30:10
	March 17	Ki Thisa	Exodus 30:11–34:35
	March 24*	VaYakhel	Exodus 35:1–38:20
	March 24	Pekudey	Exodus 38:21–40:38
	March 31	VaYikra	Leviticus 1:1–5:26
	April 7	Tzav	Leviticus 6:1–8:36
	April 21	Shemini	Leviticus 9:1–11:47
	April 28*	Tazria	Leviticus 12:1–13:59

*Two Torah portions are combined on the same Shabbat.

	SHABBAT DATE	PORTION OF THE WEEK	CITATION
	April 28	Metzorah	Leviticus 14:1–15:33
	May 5*	Acharey Moth	Leviticus 16:1–18:30
	May 5	Kedoshim	Leviticus 19:1–20:27
	May 12	Emor	Leviticus 21:1–24:23
	May 19*	BeHar	Leviticus 25:1–26:2
	May 19	BeChuko-thai	Leviticus 26:3–27:34
	May 26	BeMidbar	Numbers 1:1–4:20
	June 2	Naso	Numbers 4:21–7:89
	June 9	BeHa'alothekha	Numbers 8:1–12:16
	June 16	Sh'lach	Numbers 13:1–15:41
	June 23	Korach	Numbers 16:1–18:32
	June 30	Chukath	Numbers 19:1–22:1
	July 7	Balak	Numbers 22:2–25:9
	July 14	Pinchas	Numbers 25:10–30:1
	July 21*	Mattoth	Numbers 30:2–32:42
	July 21	Massey	Numbers 33:1–36:13
	July 28	Devarim	Deuteronomy 1:1–3:22
	August 4	VeEthChanan	Deuteronomy 3:23–7:11
	August 11	Ekev	Deuteronomy 7:12–11:25
	August 18	Re'eh	Deuteronomy 11:26–16:17
	August 25	Shof'tim	Deuteronomy 16:18–21:9
	September 1	Ki Thetze	Deuteronomy 21:10–25:18
	September 8	Ki Thavo	Deuteronomy 26:1–29:8
	September 15*	Netzavim	Deuteronomy 29:9–30:20
	September 15	VaYelekh	Deuteronomy 31:1–31:30
	September 22	HaAzinu	Deuteronomy 32:1–32:52

*Two Torah portions are combined on the same Shabbat.

	SHABBAT DATE	PORTION OF THE WEEK	CITATION
	October 12†	VeZoth HaBerakhah	Deuteronomy 33:1–34:12
	October 13	Bereshith	Genesis 1:1–6:8
	October 20	Noah	Genesis 6:9–11:32
	October 27	Lekh Lekha	Genesis 12:1–17:27
	November 3	VaYera	Genesis 18:1–22:24
	November 10	Chayay Sarah	Genesis 23:1–25:18
	November 17	Toledoth	Genesis 25:19–28:9
	November 24	VaYetze	Genesis 28:10–32:3
	December 1	VaYishlach	Genesis 32:4–36:43
	December 8	VaYeshev	Genesis 37:1–40:23
	December 15	MiKetz	Genesis 41:1–44:17
	December 22	VaYigash	Genesis 44:18–47:27
	December 29	VaYechi	Genesis 47:28–50:26
1991	January 5	Shemoth	Exodus 1:1–6:1
	January 12	VaEra	Exodus 6:2–9:35
	January 19	Bo	Exodus 10:1–13:16
	January 26	BeShalach	Exodus 13:17–17:16
	February 2	Yithro	Exodus 18:1–20:23
	February 9	Mishpatim	Exodus 21:1–24:18
	February 16	Terumah	Exodus 25:1–27:19
	February 23	Tetzaveh	Exodus 27:20–30:10
	March 2	Ki Thisa	Exodus 30:11–34:35
	March 9*	VaYakhel	Exodus 35:1–38:20
	March 9	Pekudey	Exodus 38:21–40:38
	March 16	VaYikra	Leviticus 1:1–5:26

†The final chapter of the Torah is read on Simchat Torah, which may occur other than on a Shabbat.

*Two Torah portions are combined on the same Shabbat.

	SHABBAT DATE	PORTION OF THE WEEK	CITATION
	March 23	Tzav	Leviticus 6:1–8:36
	April 13	Shemini	Leviticus 9:1–11:47
	April 20*	Tazria	Leviticus 12:1–13:59
	April 20	Metzorah	Leviticus 14:1–15:33
	April 27*	Acharey Moth	Leviticus 16:1–18:30
	April 27	Kedoshim	Leviticus 19:1–20:27
	May 4	Emor	Leviticus 21:1–24:23
	May 11*	BeHar	Leviticus 25:1–26:2
	May 11	BeChuko-thai	Leviticus 26:3–27:34
	May 18	BeMidbar	Numbers 1:1–4:20
	May 25	Naso	Numbers 4:21–7:89
	June 1	BeHa'alothekha	Numbers 8:1–12:16
	June 8	Sh'lach	Numbers 13:1–15:41
	June 15	Korach	Numbers 16:1–18:32
	June 22	Chukath	Numbers 19:1–22:1
	June 29	Balak	Numbers 22:2–25:9
	July 6	Pinchas	Numbers 25:10–30:1
	July 13*	Mattoth	Numbers 30:2–32:42
	July 13	Massey	Numbers 33:1–36:13
	July 20	Devarim	Deuteronomy 1:1–3:22
	July 27	VeEthChanan	Deuteronomy 3:23–7:11
	August 3	Ekev	Deuteronomy 7:12–11:25
	August 10	Re'eh	Deuteronomy 11:26–16:17
	August 17	Shof'tim	Deuteronomy 16:18–21:9
	August 24	Ki Thetze	Deuteronomy 21:10–25:18
	August 31	Ki Thavo	Deuteronomy 26:1–29:8

*Two Torah portions are combined on the same Shabbat.

	SHABBAT DATE	PORTION OF THE WEEK	CITATION
	September 7	Netzavim	Deuteronomy 29:9–30:20
	September 14	VaYelekh	Deuteronomy 31:1–31:30
	September 21	HaAzinu	Deuteronomy 32:1–32:52
	October 1†	VeZoth HaBerakhah	Deuteronomy 33:1–34:12
	October 5	Bereshith	Genesis 1:1–6:8
	October 12	Noah	Genesis 6:9–11:32
	October 19	Lekh Lekha	Genesis 12:1–17:27
	October 26	VaYera	Genesis 18:1–22:24
	November 2	Chayay Sarah	Genesis 23:1–25:18
	November 9	Toledoth	Genesis 25:19–28:9
	November 16	VaYetze	Genesis 28:10–32:3
	November 23	VaYishlach	Genesis 32:4–36:43
	November 30	VaYeshev	Genesis 37:1–40:23
	December 7	MiKetz	Genesis 41:1–44:17
	December 14	VaYigash	Genesis 44:18–47:27
	December 21	VaYechi	Genesis 47:28–50:26
	December 28	Shemot	Exodus 1:1–6:1
1992	January 4	VaEra	Exodus 6:2–9:35
	January 11	Bo	Exodus 10:1–13:16
	January 18	BeShalach	Exodus 13:17–17:16
	January 25	Yithro	Exodus 18:1–20:23
	February 1	Mishpatim	Exodus 21:1–24:18
	February 8	Terumah	Exodus 25:1–27:19
	February 15	Tetzaveh	Exodus 27:20–30:10
	February 22	Ki Thisa	Exodus 30:11–34:35
	February 29	VaYakhel	Exodus 35:1–38:20

† The final chapter of the Torah is read on Simchat Torah, which may occur other than on a Shabbat.

	SHABBAT DATE	PORTION OF THE WEEK	CITATION
	March 7	Pekudey	Exodus 38:21–40:38
	March 14	VaYikra	Leviticus 1:1–5:26
	March 21	Tzav	Leviticus 6:1–8:36
	March 28	Shemini	Leviticus 9:1–11:47
	April 4	Tazria	Leviticus 12:1–13:59
	April 11	Metzorah	Leviticus 14:1–15:33
	May 2	Acharey Moth	Leviticus 16:1–18:30
	May 9	Kedoshim	Leviticus 19:1–20:27
	May 16	Emor	Leviticus 21:1–24:23
	May 23	BeHar	Leviticus 25:1–26:2
	May 30	BeChuko-thai	Leviticus 26:3–27:34
	June 6	BeMidbar	Numbers 1:1–4:20
	June 13	Naso	Numbers 4:21–7:89
	June 20	BeHa'alothekha	Numbers 8:1–12:16
	June 27	Sh'lach	Numbers 13:1–15:41
	July 4	Korach	Numbers 16:1–18:32
	July 11	Chukath	Numbers 19:1–22:1
	July 18	Balak	Numbers 22:2–25:9
	July 25	Pinchas	Numbers 25:10–30:1
	August 1*	Mattoth	Numbers 30:2–32:42
	August 1	Massey	Numbers 33:1–36:13
	August 8	Devarim	Deuteronomy 1:1–3:22
	August 15	VeEthChanan	Deuteronomy 3:23–7:11
	August 22	Ekev	Deuteronomy 7:12–11:25
	August 29	Re'eh	Deuteronomy 11:26–16:17
	September 5	Shof'tim	Deuteronomy 16:18–21:9

*Two Torah portions are combined on the same Shabbat.

	SHABBAT DATE	PORTION OF THE WEEK	CITATION
	September 12	Ki Thetze	Deuteronomy 21:10–25:18
	September 19	Ki Thavo	Deuteronomy 26:1–29:8
	September 26	Netzavim	Deuteronomy 29:9–30:20
	October 3	VaYelekh	Deuteronomy 31:1–31:30
	October 10	HaAzinu	Deuteronomy 32:1–32:52
	October 20†	VeZoth HaBerakhah	Deuteronomy 33:1–34:12
	October 24	Bereshith	Genesis 1:1–6:8
	October 31	Noah	Genesis 6:9–11:32
	November 7	Lekh Lekha	Genesis 12:1–17:27
	November 14	VaYera	Genesis 18:1–22:24
	November 21	Chayay Sarah	Genesis 23:1–25:18
	November 28	Toledoth	Genesis 25:19–28:9
	December 5	VaYetze	Genesis 28:10–32:3
	December 12	VaYishlach	Genesis 32:4–36:43
	December 19	VaYeshev	Genesis 37:1–40:23
	December 26	MiKetz	Genesis 41:1–44:17
1993	January 2	VaYigash	Genesis 44:18–47:27
	January 9	VaYechi	Genesis 47:28–50:26
	January 16	Shemoth	Exodus 1:1–6:1
	January 23	VaEra	Exodus 6:2–9:35
	January 30	Bo	Exodus 10:1–13:16
	February 6	BeShalach	Exodus 13:17–17:16
	February 13	Yithro	Exodus 18:1–20:23
	February 20	Mishpatim	Exodus 21:1–24:18
	February 27	Terumah	Exodus 25:1–27:19
	March 6	Tetzaveh	Exodus 27:20–30:10

†The final chapter of the Torah is read on Simchat Torah, which may occur other than on a Shabbat.

	SHABBAT DATE	PORTION OF THE WEEK	CITATION
	March 13	Ki Thisa	Exodus 30:11–34:35
	March 20*	VaYakhel	Exodus 35:1–38:20
	March 20	Pekudey	Exodus 38:21–40:38
	March 27	VaYikra	Leviticus 1:1–5:26
	April 3	Tzav	Leviticus 6:1–8:36
	April 17	Shemini	Leviticus 9:1–11:47
	April 24*	Tazria	Leviticus 12:1–13:59
	April 24	Metzorah	Leviticus 14:1–15:33
	May 1*	Acharey Moth	Leviticus 16:1–18:30
	May 1	Kedoshim	Leviticus 19:1–20:27
	May 8	Emor	Leviticus 21:1–24:23
	May 15*	BeHar	Leviticus 25:1–26:2
	May 15	BeChuko-thai	Leviticus 26:3–27:34
	May 22	BeMidbar	Numbers 1:1–4:20
	May 29	Naso	Numbers 4:21–7:89
	June 5	BeHa'alothekha	Numbers 8:1–12:16
	June 12	Sh'lach	Numbers 13:1–15:41
	June 19	Korach	Numbers 16:1–18:32
	June 26	Chukath	Numbers 19:1–22:1
	July 3	Balak	Numbers 22:2–25:9
	July 10	Pinchas	Numbers 25:10–30:1
	July 17*	Mattoth	Numbers 30:2–32:42
	July 17	Massey	Numbers 33:1–36:13
	July 24	Devarim	Deuteronomy 1:1–3:22
	July 31	VeEthChanan	Deuteronomy 3:23–7:11
	August 7	Ekev	Deuteronomy 7:12–11:25

*Two Torah portions are combined on the same Shabbat.

	SHABBAT DATE	PORTION OF THE WEEK	CITATION
	August 14	Re'eh	Deuteronomy 11:26–16:17
	August 21	Shof'tim	Deuteronomy 16:18–21:9
	August 28	Ki Thetze	Deuteronomy 21:10–25:18
	September 4	Ki Thavo	Deuteronomy 26:1–29:8
	September 11*	Netzavim	Deuteronomy 29:9–30:20
	September 11	VaYelekh	Deuteronomy 31:1–31:30
	September 18	HaAzinu	Deuteronomy 32:1–32:52
	October 8†	VeZoth HaBerakhah	Deuteronomy 33:1–34:12
	October 9	Bereshith	Genesis 1:1–6:8
	October 16	Noah	Genesis 6:9–11:32
	October 23	Lekh Lekha	Genesis 12:1–17:27
	October 30	VaYera	Genesis 18:1–22:24
	November 6	Chayay Sarah	Genesis 23:1–25:18
	November 13	Toledoth	Genesis 25:19–28:9
	November 20	VaYetze	Genesis 28:10–32:3
	November 27	VaYishlach	Genesis 32:4–36:43
	December 4	VaYeshev	Genesis 37:1–40:23
	December 11	MiKetz	Genesis 41:1–44:17
	December 18	VaYigash	Genesis 44:18–47:27
	December 25	VaYechi	Genesis 47–50:26
1994	January 1	Shemoth	Exodus 1:1–6:1
	January 8	VaEra	Exodus 6:2–9:35
	January 15	Bo	Exodus 10:1–13:16
	January 22	BeShalach	Exodus 13:17–17:16
	January 29	Yithro	Exodus 18:1–20:23

*Two Torah portions are combined on the same Shabbat.
†The final chapter of the Torah is read on Simchat Torah, which may occur other than on a Shabbat.

SHABBAT DATE	PORTION OF THE WEEK	CITATION
February 5	Mishpatim	Exodus 21:1–24:18
February 12	Terumah	Exodus 25:1–27:19
February 19	Tetzaveh	Exodus 27:20–30:10
February 26	Ki Thisa	Exodus 30:11–34:35
March 5	VaYakhel	Exodus 35:1–38:20
March 12	Pekudey	Exodus 38:21–40:38
March 19	VaYikra	Leviticus 1:1–5:26
March 26	Tzav	Leviticus 6:1–8:36
April 9	Shemini	Leviticus 9:1–11:47
April 16*	Tazria	Leviticus 12:1–13:59
April 16	Metzorah	Leviticus 14:1–15:33
April 23*	Acharey Moth	Leviticus 16:1–18:30
April 23	Kedoshim	Leviticus 19:1–20:27
April 30	Emor	Leviticus 21:1–24:23
May 7*	BeHar	Leviticus 25:1–26:2
May 7	BeChuko-thai	Leviticus 26:3–27:34
May 14	BeMidbar	Numbers 1:1–4:20
May 21	Naso	Numbers 4:21–7:89
May 28	BeHa'alothekha	Numbers 8:1–12:16
June 4	Sh'lach	Numbers 13:1–15:41
June 11	Korach	Numbers 16:1–18:32
June 18	Chukath	Numbers 19:1–22:1
June 25	Balak	Numbers 22:2–25:9
July 2	Pinchas	Numbers 25:10–30:1
July 9*	Mattoth	Numbers 30:2–32:42
July 9*	Massey	Numbers 33:1–36:13

*Two Torah portions are combined on the same Shabbat.

	SHABBAT DATE	PORTION OF THE WEEK	CITATION
	July 16	Devarim	Deuteronomy 1:1–3:22
	July 23	VeEthChanan	Deuteronomy 3:23–7:11
	July 30	Ekev	Deuteronomy 7:12–11:25
	August 6	Re'eh	Deuteronomy 11:26–16:17
	August 13	Shof'tim	Deuteronomy 16:18–21:9
	August 20	Ki Thetze	Deuteronomy 21:10–25:18
	August 27	Ki Thavo	Deuteronomy 26:1–29:8
	September 3	Netzavim	Deuteronomy 29:9–30:20
	September 10	VaYelekh	Deuteronomy 31:1–31:30
	September 17	HaAzinu	Deuteronomy 32:1–32:52
	September 28[†]	VeZoth HaBerakhah	Deuteronomy 33:1–34:12
	October 1	Bereshith	Genesis 1:1–6:8
	October 8	Noah	Genesis 6:9–11:32
	October 15	Lekh Lekha	Genesis 12:1–17:27
	October 22	VaYera	Genesis 18:1–22:24
	October 29	Chayay Sarah	Genesis 23:1–25:18
	November 5	Toledoth	Genesis 25:19–28:9
	November 12	VaYetze	Genesis 28:10–32:3
	November 19	VaYishlach	Genesis 32:4–36:43
	November 26	VaYeshev	Genesis 37:1–40:23
	December 3	MiKetz	Genesis 41:1–44:17
	December 10	VaYigash	Genesis 44:18–47:27
	December 17	VaYechi	Genesis 47:28–50:26
	December 24	Shemot	Exodus 1:1–6:1
	December 31	VaEra	Exodus 6:2–9:35
1995	January 7	Bo	Exodus 10:1–13:16

[†] The final chapter of the Torah is read on Simchat Torah, which may occur other than on a Shabbat.

SHABBAT DATE	PORTION OF THE WEEK	CITATION
January 14	BeShalach	Exodus 13:17–17:16
January 21	Yithro	Exodus 18:1–20:23
January 28	Mishpatim	Exodus 21:1–24:18
February 4	Terumah	Exodus 25:1–27:19
February 11	Tetzaveh	Exodus 27:20–30:10
February 18	Ki Thisa	Exodus 30:11–34:35
February 25	VaYakhel	Exodus 35:1–38:20
March 4	Pekudey	Exodus 38:21–40:38
March 11	VaYikra	Leviticus 1:1–5:26
March 18	Tzav	Leviticus 6:1–8:36
March 25	Shemini	Leviticus 9:1–11:47
April 1	Tazria	Leviticus 12:1–13:59
April 8	Metzorah	Leviticus 14:1–15:33
April 29	Acharey Moth	Leviticus 16:1–18:30
May 6	Kedoshim	Leviticus 19:1–20:27
May 13	Emor	Leviticus 21:1–24:23
May 20	BeHar	Leviticus 25:1–26:2
May 27	BeChuko-thai	Leviticus 26:3–27:34
June 3	BeMidbar	Numbers 1:1–4:20
June 10	Naso	Numbers 4:21–7:89
June 17	BeHa'alothekha	Numbers 8:1–12:16
June 24	Sh'lach	Numbers 13:1–15:41
July 1	Korach	Numbers 16:1–18:32
July 8	Chukath	Numbers 19:1–22:1
July 15	Balak	Numbers 22:2–25:9
July 22	Pinchas	Numbers 25:10–30:1

SHABBAT DATE	PORTION OF THE WEEK	CITATION
July 29*	Mattoth	Numbers 30:2–32:42
July 29	Massey	Numbers 33:1–36:13
August 5	Devarim	Deuteronomy 1:1–3:22
August 12	VeEthChanan	Deuteronomy 3:23–7:11
August 19	Ekev	Deuteronomy 7:12–11:25
August 26	Re'eh	Deuteronomy 11:26–16:17
September 2	Shof'tim	Deuteronomy 16:18–21:9
September 9	Ki Thetze	Deuteronomy 21:10–25:18
September 16	Ki Thavo	Deuteronomy 26:1–29:8
September 23	Netzavim	Deuteronomy 29:9–30:20
September 30	VaYelekh	Deuteronomy 31:1–31:30
October 7	HaAzinu	Deuteronomy 32:1–32:52
October 17†	VeZoth HaBerakhah	Deuteronomy 33:1–34:12
October 21	Bereshith	Genesis 1:1–6:8
October 28	Noah	Genesis 6:9–11:32
November 4	Lekh Lekha	Genesis 12:1–17:27
November 11	VaYera	Genesis 18:1–22:24
November 18	Chayay Sarah	Genesis 23:1–25:18
November 25	Toledoth	Genesis 25:19–28:9
December 2	VaYetze	Genesis 28:10–32:3
December 9	VaYishlach	Genesis 32:4–36:43
December 16	VaYeshev	Genesis 37:1–40:23
December 23	MiKetz	Genesis 41:1–44:17
December 30	VaYigash	Genesis 44:18–47:27

*Two Torah portions are combined on the same Shabbat.
†The final chapter of the Torah is read on Simchat Torah, which may occur other than on a Shabbat.

	SHABBAT DATE	PORTION OF THE WEEK	CITATION
1996	January 6	VaYechi	Genesis 47:28–50:26
	January 13	Shemoth	Exodus 1:1–6:1
	January 20	VaEra	Exodus 6:2–9:35
	January 27	Bo	Exodus 10:1–13:16
	February 3	BeShalach	Exodus 13:17–17:16
	February 10	Yithro	Exodus 18:1–20:23
	February 17	Mishpatim	Exodus 21:1–24:18
	February 24	Terumah	Exodus 25:1–27:19
	March 2	Tetzaveh	Exodus 27:20–30:10
	March 9	Ki Thisa	Exodus 30:11–34:35
	March 16*	VaYakhel	Exodus 35:1–38:20
	March 16	Pekudey	Exodus 38:21–40:38
	March 23	VaYikra	Leviticus 1:1–5:26
	March 30	Tzav	Leviticus 6:1–8:36
	April 13	Shemini	Leviticus 9:1–11:47
	April 20*	Tazria	Leviticus 12:1–13:59
	April 20	Metzorah	Leviticus 14:1–15:33
	April 27*	Acharey Moth	Leviticus 16:1–18:30
	April 27*	Kedoshim	Leviticus 19:1–20:27
	May 4	Emor	Leviticus 21:1–24:23
	May 11*	BeHar	Leviticus 25:1–26:2
	May 11	BeChuko-thai	Leviticus 26:3–27:34
	May 18	BeMidbar	Numbers 1:1–4:20
	June 1	Naso	Numbers 4:21–7:89
	June 8	BeHa'alothekha	Numbers 8:1–12:16
	June 15	Sh'lach	Numbers 13:1–15:41

*Two Torah portions are combined on the same Shabbat.

	SHABBAT DATE	PORTION OF THE WEEK	CITATION
	June 22	Korach	Numbers 16:1–18:32
	June 29*	Chukath	Numbers 19:1–22:1
	June 29	Balak	Numbers 22:2–25:9
	July 6	Pinchas	Numbers 25:10–30:1
	July 13*	Mattoth	Numbers 30:2–32:42
	July 13	Massey	Numbers 33:1–36:13
	July 20	Devarim	Deuteronomy 1:1–3:22
	July 27	VeEthChanan	Deuteronomy 3:23–7:11
	August 3	Ekev	Deuteronomy 7:12–11:25
	August 10	Re'eh	Deuteronomy 11:26–16:17
	August 17	Shof'tim	Deuteronomy 16:18–21:9
	August 24	Ki Thetze	Deuteronomy 21:10–25:18
	August 31	Ki Thavo	Deuteronomy 26:1–29:8
	September 7*	Netzavim	Deuteronomy 29:9–30:20
	September 7	VaYelekh	Deuteronomy 31:1–31:30
	September 21	HaAzinu	Deuteronomy 32:1–32:52
	October 6†	VeZoth HaBerakhah	Deuteronomy 33:1–34:12
	October 12	Bereshith	Genesis 1:1–6:8
	October 19	Noah	Genesis 6:9–11:32
	October 26	Lekh Lekha	Genesis 12:1–17:27
	November 2	VaYera	Genesis 18:1–22:24
	November 9	Chayay Sarah	Genesis 23:1–25:18
	November 16	Toledoth	Genesis 25:19–28:9
	November 23	VaYetze	Genesis 28:10–32:3
	November 30	VaYishlach	Genesis 32:4–36:43

*Two Torah portions are combined on the same Shabbat.
†The final chapter of the Torah is read on Simchat Torah, which may occur other than on a Shabbat.

	SHABBAT DATE	PORTION OF THE WEEK	CITATION
	December 7	VaYeshev	Genesis 37:1–40:23
	December 14	MiKetz	Genesis 41:1–44:17
	December 21	VaYigash	Genesis 44:18–47:27
	December 28	VaYechi	Genesis 47:28–50:26
1997	January 4	Shemoth	Exodus 1:1–6:1
	January 11	VaEra	Exodus 6:2–9:35
	January 18	Bo	Exodus 10:1–13:16
	January 25	BeShalach	Exodus 13:17–17:16
	February 1	Yithro	Exodus 18:1–20:23
	February 8	Mishpatim	Exodus 21:1–24:18
	February 15	Terumah	Exodus 25:1–27:19
	February 22	Tetzaveh	Exodus 27:20–30:10
	March 1	Ki Thisa	Exodus 30:11–34:35
	March 8	VaYakhel	Exodus 35:1–38:20
	March 15	Pekudey	Exodus 38:21–40:38
	March 22	VaYikra	Leviticus 1:1–5:26
	March 29	Tzav	Leviticus 6:1–8:36
	April 5	Shemini	Leviticus 9:1–11:47
	April 12	Tazria	Leviticus 12:1–13:59
	April 19	Metzorah	Leviticus 14:1–15:33
	May 3	Acharey Moth	Leviticus 16:1–18:30
	May 10	Kedoshim	Leviticus 19:1–20:27
	May 17	Emor	Leviticus 21:1–24:23
	May 24	BeHar	Leviticus 25:1–26:2
	May 31	BeChuko-thai	Leviticus 26:3–27:34
	June 7	BeMidbar	Numbers 1:1–4:20
	June 14	Naso	Numbers 4:21–7:89

	SHABBAT DATE	PORTION OF THE WEEK	CITATION
	June 21	BeHa'alothekha	Numbers 8:1–12:16
	June 28	Sh'lach	Numbers 13:1–15:41
	July 5	Korach	Numbers 16:1–18:32
	July 12	Chukath	Numbers 19:1–22:1
	July 19	Balak	Numbers 22:2–25:9
	July 26	Pinchas	Numbers 25:10–30:1
	August 2*	Mattoth	Numbers 30:2–32:42
	August 2	Massey	Numbers 33:1–36:13
	August 9	Devarim	Deuteronomy 1:1–3:22
	August 16	VeEthChanan	Deuteronomy 3:23–7:11
	August 23	Ekev	Deuteronomy 7:12–11:25
	August 30	Re'eh	Deuteronomy 11:26–16:17
	September 6	Shof'tim	Deuteronomy 16:18–21:9
	September 13	Ki Thetze	Deuteronomy 21:10–25:18
	September 20	Ki Thavo	Deuteronomy 26:1–29:8
	September 27*	Netzavim	Deuteronomy 29:9–30:20
	September 27	VaYelekh	Deuteronomy 31:1–31:30
	October 4	HaAzinu	Deuteronomy 32:1–32:52
	October 24†	VeZoth HaBerakhah	Deuteronomy 33:1–34:12
	October 25	Bereshith	Genesis 1:1–6:8
	November 1	Noah	Genesis 6:9–11:32
	November 8	Lekh Lekha	Genesis 12:1–17:27
	November 15	VaYera	Genesis 18:1–22:24
	November 22	Chayay Sarah	Genesis 23:1–25:18
	November 29	Toledoth	Genesis 25:19–28:9

*Two Torah portions are combined on the same Shabbat.
†The final chapter of the Torah is read on Simchat Torah, which may occur other than on a Shabbat.

	SHABBAT DATE	PORTION OF THE WEEK	CITATION
	December 6	VaYetze	Genesis 28:10–32:3
	December 13	VaYishlach	Genesis 32:4–36:43
	December 20	VaYeshev	Genesis 37:1–40:23
	December 27	MiKetz	Genesis 41:1–44:17
1998	January 3	VaYigash	Genesis 44:18–47:27
	January 10	VaYechi	Genesis 47:28–50:26
	January 17	Shemoth	Exodus 1:1–6:1
	January 24	VaEra	Exodus 6:2–9:35
	January 31	Bo	Exodus 10:1–13:16
	February 7	BeShalach	Exodus 13:17–17:16
	February 14	Yithro	Exodus 18:1–20:23
	February 21	Mishpatim	Exodus 21:1–24:18
	February 28	Terumah	Exodus 25:1–27:19
	March 7	Tetzaveh	Exodus 27:20–30:10
	March 14	Ki Thisa	Exodus 30:11–34:35
	March 21*	VaYakhel	Exodus 35:1–38:20
	March 21	Pekudey	Exodus 38:21–40:38
	March 28	VaYikra	Leviticus 1:1–5:26
	April 4	Tzav	Leviticus 6:1–8:36
	April 25	Shemini	Leviticus 9:1–11:47
	May 2*	Tazria	Leviticus 12:1–13:59
	May 2	Metzorah	Leviticus 14:1–15:33
	May 9*	Acharey Moth	Leviticus 16:1–18:30
	May 9	Kedoshim	Leviticus 19:1–20:27
	May 16	Emor	Leviticus 21:1–24:23
	May 23*	BeHar	Leviticus 25:1–26:2

*Two Torah portions are combined on the same Shabbat.

SHABBAT DATE	PORTION OF THE WEEK	CITATION
May 23	BeChuko-thai	Leviticus 26:3–27:34
May 30	BeMidbar	Numbers 1:1–4:20
June 6	Naso	Numbers 4:21–7:89
June 13	BeHa'alothekha	Numbers 8:1–12:16
June 20	Sh'lach	Numbers 13:1–15:41
June 27	Korach	Numbers 16:1–18:32
July 4	Chukath	Numbers 19:1–22:1
July 11	Balak	Numbers 22:2–25:9
July 18	Pinchas	Numbers 25:10–30:1
July 25*	Mattoth	Numbers 30:2–32:42
July 25	Massey	Numbers 33:1–36:13
August 1	Devarim	Deuteronomy 1:1–3:22
August 8	VeEthChanan	Deuteronomy 3:23–7:11
August 15	Ekev	Deuteronomy 7:12–11:25
August 22	Re'eh	Deuteronomy 11:26–16:17
August 29	Shof'tim	Deuteronomy 16:18–21:9
September 5	Ki Thetze	Deuteronomy 21:10–25:18
September 12	Ki Thavo	Deuteronomy 26:1–29:8
September 19	Netzavim	Deuteronomy 29:9–30:20
September 26	VaYelekh	Deuteronomy 31:1–31:30
October 3	HaAzinu	Deuteronomy 32:1–32:52
October 13†	VeZoth HaBerakhah	Deuteronomy 33:1–34:12
October 17	Bereshith	Genesis 1:1–6:8
October 24	Noah	Genesis 6:9–11:32
October 31	Lekh Lekha	Genesis 12:1–17:27

*Two Torah portions are combined on the same Shabbat.
†The final chapter of the Torah is read on Simchat Torah, which may occur other than on a Shabbat.

	SHABBAT DATE	PORTION OF THE WEEK	CITATION
	November 7	VaYera	Genesis 18:1–22:24
	November 14	Chayay Sarah	Genesis 23:1–25:18
	November 21	Toledoth	Genesis 25:19–28:9
	November 28	VaYetze	Genesis 28:10–32:3
	December 5	VaYishlach	Genesis 32:4–36:43
	December 12	VaYeshev	Genesis 37:1–40:23
	December 19	MiKetz	Genesis 41:1–44:17
	December 26	VaYigash	Genesis 44:18–47:27
1999	January 2	VaYechi	Genesis 47:28–50:26
	January 9	Shemoth	Exodus 1:1–6:1
	January 16	VaEra	Exodus 6:2–9:35
	January 23	Bo	Exodus 10:1–13:16
	January 30	BeShalach	Exodus 13:17–17:16
	February 6	Yithro	Exodus 18:1–20:23
	February 13	Mishpatim	Exodus 21:1–24:18
	February 20	Terumah	Exodus 25:1–27:19
	February 27	Tetzaveh	Exodus 27:20–30:10
	March 6	Ki Thisa	Exodus 30:11–34:35
	March 13*	VaYakhel	Exodus 35:1–38:20
	March 13	Pekudey	Exodus 38:21–40:38
	March 20	VaYikra	Leviticus 1:1–5:26
	March 27	Tzav	Leviticus 6:1–8:36
	April 10	Shemini	Leviticus 9:1–11:47
	April 17*	Tazria	Leviticus 12:1–13:59
	April 17	Metzorah	Leviticus 14:1–15:33
	April 24*	Acharey Moth	Leviticus 16:1–18:30

*Two Torah portions are combined on the same Shabbat.

	SHABBAT DATE	PORTION OF THE WEEK	CITATION
	April 24	Kedoshim	Leviticus 19:1–20:27
	May 1	Emor	Leviticus 21:1–24:23
	May 8	BeHar	Leviticus 25:1–26:2
	May 15	BeChuko-thai	Leviticus 26:3–27:34
	May 22	BeMidbar	Numbers 1:1–4:20
	May 29	Naso	Numbers 4:21–7:89
	June 5	BeHa'alothekha	Numbers 8:1–12:16
	June 12	Sh'lach	Numbers 13:1–15:41
	June 19	Korach	Numbers 16:1–18:32
	June 26*	Chukath	Numbers 19:1–22:1
	June 26	Balak	Numbers 22:2–25:9
	July 3	Pinchas	Numbers 25:10–30:1
	July 10*	Mattoth	Numbers 30:2–32:42
	July 10	Massey	Numbers 33:1–36:13
	July 17	Devarim	Deuteronomy 1:1–3:22
	July 24	VeEthChanan	Deuteronomy 3:23–7:11
	July 31	Ekev	Deuteronomy 7:12–11:25
	August 7	Re'eh	Deuteronomy 11:26–16:17
	August 14	Shof'tim	Deuteronomy 16:18–21:9
	August 21	Ki Thetze	Deuteronomy 21:10–25:18
	August 28	Ki Thavo	Deuteronomy 26:1–29:8
	September 4*	Netzavim	Deuteronomy 29:9–30:20
	September 4	VaYelekh	Deuteronomy 31:1–31:30
	September 18	HaAzinu	Deuteronomy 32:1–32:52
	October 3†	VeZoth HaBerakhah	Deuteronomy 33:1–34:12

*Two Torah portions are combined on the same Shabbat.
†The final chapter of the Torah is read on Simchat Torah, which may occur other than on a Shabbat.

	SHABBAT DATE	PORTION OF THE WEEK	CITATION
	October 9	Bereshith	Genesis 1:1–6:8
	October 16	Noah	Genesis 6:9–11:32
	October 23	Lekh Lekha	Genesis 12:1–17:27
	October 30	VaYera	Genesis 18:1–22:24
	November 6	Chayay Sarah	Genesis 23:1–25:18
	November 13	Toledoth	Genesis 25:19–28:9
	November 20	VaYetze	Genesis 28:10–32:3
	November 27	VaYishlach	Genesis 32:4–36:43
	December 4	VaYeshev	Genesis 37:1–40:23
	December 11	MiKetz	Genesis 41:1–44:17
	December 18	VaYigash	Genesis 44:18–47:27
	December 25	VaYechi	Genesis 47:28–50:26
2000	January 1	Shemoth	Exodus 1:1–6:1
	January 8	VaEra	Exodus 6:2–9:35
	January 15	Bo	Exodus 10:1–13:16
	January 22	BeShalach	Exodus 13:17–17:16
	January 29	Yithro	Exodus 18:1–20:23
	February 5	Mishpatim	Exodus 21:1–24:18
	February 12	Terumah	Exodus 25:1–27:19
	February 19	Tetzaveh	Exodus 27:20–30:10
	February 26	Ki Thisa	Exodus 30:11–34:35
	March 4	VaYakhel	Exodus 35:1–38:20
	March 11	Pekudey	Exodus 38:21–40:38
	March 18	VaYikra	Leviticus 1:1–5:26
	March 25	Tzav	Leviticus 6:1–8:36
	April 1	Shemini	Leviticus 9:1–11:47
	April 8	Tazria	Leviticus 12:1–13:59

	SHABBAT DATE	PORTION OF THE WEEK	CITATION
	April 15	Metzorah	Leviticus 14:1–15:33
	April 29	Acharey Moth	Leviticus 16:1–18:30
	May 6	Kedoshim	Leviticus 19:1–20:27
	May 13	Emor	Leviticus 21:1–24:23
	May 20	BeHar	Leviticus 25:1–26:2
	May 27	BeChuko-thai	Leviticus 26:3–27:34
	June 3	BeMidbar	Numbers 1:1–4:20
	June 17	Naso	Numbers 4:21–7:89
	June 24	BeHa'alothekha	Numbers 8:1–12:16
	July 1	Sh'lach	Numbers 13:1–15:41
	July 8	Korach	Numbers 16:1–18:32
	July 15*	Chukath	Numbers 19:1–22:1
	July 15	Balak	Numbers 22:2–25:9
	July 22	Pinchas	Numbers 25:10–30:1
	July 29*	Mattoth	Numbers 30:2–32:42
	July 29	Massey	Numbers 33:1–36:13
	August 5	Devarim	Deuteronomy 1:1–3:22
	August 12	VeEthChanan	Deuteronomy 3:23–7:11
	August 19	Ekev	Deuteronomy 7:12–11:25
	August 26	Re'eh	Deuteronomy 11:26–16:17
	September 2	Shof'tim	Deuteronomy 16:18–21:9
	September 9	Ki Thetze	Deuteronomy 21:10–25:18
	September 16	Ki Thavo	Deuteronomy 26:1–29:8
	September 23*	Netzavim	Deuteronomy 29:9–30:20
	September 23	VaYelekh	Deuteronomy 31:1–31:30
	October 7	HaAzinu	Deuteronomy 32:1–32:52

*Two Torah portions are combined on the same Shabbat.

	SHABBAT DATE	PORTION OF THE WEEK	CITATION
	October 22[†]	VeZoth HaBerakhah	Deuteronomy 33:1–34:12
	October 28	Bereshith	Genesis 1:1–6:8
	November 4	Noah	Genesis 6:9–11:32
	November 11	Lekh Lekha	Genesis 12:1–17:27
	November 18	VaYera	Genesis 18:1–22:24
	November 25	Chayay Sarah	Genesis 23:1–25:18
	December 2	Toledoth	Genesis 25:19–28:9
	December 9	VaYetze	Genesis 28:10–32:3
	December 16	VaYishlach	Genesis 32:4–36:43
	December 23	VaYeshev	Genesis 37:1–40:23
	December 30	MiKetz	Genesis 41:1–44:17
2001	January 6	VaYigash	Genesis 44:18–47:27
	January 13	VaYechi	Genesis 47:28–50:26
	January 20	Shemoth	Exodus 1:1–6:1
	January 27	VaEra	Exodus 6:2–9:35
	February 3	Bo	Exodus 10:1–13:16
	February 10	BeShalach	Exodus 13:17–17:16
	February 17	Yithro	Exodus 18:1–20:23
	February 24	Mishpatim	Exodus 21:1–24:18
	March 3	Terumah	Exodus 25:1–27:19
	March 10	Tetzaveh	Exodus 27:20–30:10
	March 17	Ki Thisa	Exodus 30:11–34:35
	March 24*	VaYakhel	Exodus 35:1–38:20
	March 24	Pekudey	Exodus 38:21–40:38
	March 31	VaYikra	Leviticus 1:1–5:26

[†]The final chapter of the Torah is read on Simchat Torah, which may occur other than on a Shabbat.

*Two Torah portions are combined on the same Shabbat.

SHABBAT DATE	PORTION OF THE WEEK	CITATION
April 7	Tzav	Leviticus 6:1–8:36
April 21	Shemini	Leviticus 9:1–11:47
April 28*	Tazria	Leviticus 12:1–13:59
April 28	Metzorah	Leviticus 14:1–15:33
May 5*	Acharey Moth	Leviticus 16:1–18:30
May 5	Kedoshim	Leviticus 19:1–20:27
May 12	Emor	Leviticus 21:1–24:23
May 19*	BeHar	Leviticus 25:1–26:2
May 19	BeChuko-thai	Leviticus 26:3–27:34
May 26	BeMidbar	Numbers 1:1–4:20
June 2	Naso	Numbers 4:21–7:89
June 9	BeHa'alothekha	Numbers 8:1–12:16
June 16	Sh'lach	Numbers 13:1–15:41
June 23	Korach	Numbers 16:1–18:32
June 30	Chukath	Numbers 19:1–22:1
July 7	Balak	Numbers 22:2–25:9
July 14	Pinchas	Numbers 25:10–30:1
July 21*	Mattoth	Numbers 30:2–32:42
July 21	Massey	Numbers 33:1–36:13
July 28	Devarim	Deuteronomy 1:1–3:22
August 4	VeEthChanan	Deuteronomy 3:23–7:11
August 11	Ekev	Deuteronomy 7:12–11:25
August 18	Re'eh	Deuteronomy 11:26–16:17
August 25	Shof'tim	Deuteronomy 16:18–21:9
September 1	Ki Thetze	Deuteronomy 21:10–25:18
September 8	Ki Thavo	Deuteronomy 26:1–29:8

*Two Torah portions are combined on the same Shabbat.

	SHABBAT DATE	PORTION OF THE WEEK	CITATION
	September 15	Netzavim	Deuteronomy 29:9–30:20
	September 22	VaYelekh	Deuteronomy 31:1–31:30
	September 29	HaAzinu	Deuteronomy 32:1–32:52
	October 10†	VeZoth HaBerakhah	Deuteronomy 33:1–34:12
	October 13	Bereshith	Genesis 1:1–6:8
	October 20	Noah	Genesis 6:9–11:32
	October 27	Lekh Lekha	Genesis 12:1–17:27
	November 3	VaYera	Genesis 18:1–22:24
	November 10	Chayay Sarah	Genesis 23:1–25:18
	November 17	Toledoth	Genesis 25:19–28:9
	November 24	VaYetze	Genesis 28:10–32:3
	December 1	VaYishlach	Genesis 32:4–36:43
	December 8	VaYeshev	Genesis 37:1–40:23
	December 15	MiKetz	Genesis 41:1–44:17
	December 22	VaYigash	Genesis 44:18–47:27
	December 29	VaYechi	Genesis 47:28–50:26
2002	January 5	Shemoth	Exodus 1:1–6:1
	January 12	VaEra	Exodus 6:2–9:35
	January 19	Bo	Exodus 10:1–13:16
	January 26	BeShalach	Exodus 13:17–17:16
	February 2	Yithro	Exodus 18:1–20:23
	February 9	Mishpatim	Exodus 21:1–24:18
	February 16	Terumah	Exodus 25:1–27:19
	February 23	Tetzaveh	Exodus 27:20–30:10
	March 2	Ki Thisa	Exodus 30:11–34:35
	March 9*	VaYakhel	Exodus 35:1–38:20

†The final chapter of the Torah is read on Simchat Torah, which may occur other than on a Shabbat.

*Two Torah portions are combined on the same Shabbat.

	SHABBAT DATE	PORTION OF THE WEEK	CITATION
	March 9	Pekudey	Exodus 38:21–40:38
	March 16	VaYikra	Leviticus 1:1–5:26
	March 23	Tzav	Leviticus 6:1–8:36
	April 6	Shemini	Leviticus 9:1–11:47
	April 13*	Tazria	Leviticus 12:1–13:59
	April 13	Metzorah	Leviticus 14:1–15:33
	April 20*	Acharey Moth	Leviticus 16:1–18:30
	April 20	Kedoshim	Leviticus 19:1–20:27
	April 27	Emor	Leviticus 21:1–24:23
	May 4*	BeHar	Leviticus 25:1–26:2
	May 4	BeChuko-thai	Leviticus 26:3–27:34
	May 11	BeMidbar	Numbers 1:1–4:20
	May 25	Naso	Numbers 4:21–7:89
	June 1	BeHa'alothekha	Numbers 8:1–12:16
	June 8	Sh'lach	Numbers 13:1–15:41
	June 15	Korach	Numbers 16:1–18:32
	June 22*	Chukath	Numbers 19:1–22:1
	June 22	Balak	Numbers 22:2–25:9
	June 29	Pinchas	Numbers 25:10–30:1
	July 6*	Mattoth	Numbers 30:2–32:42
	July 6	Massey	Numbers 33:1–36:13
	July 13	Devarim	Deuteronomy 1:1–3:22
	July 20	VeEthChanan	Deuteronomy 3:23–7:11
	July 27	Ekev	Deuteronomy 7:12–11:25
	August 3	Re'eh	Deuteronomy 11:26–16:17
	August 10	Shof'tim	Deuteronomy 16:18–21:9
	August 17	Ki Thetze	Deuteronomy 21:10–25:18

*Two Torah portions are combined on the same Shabbat.

	SHABBAT DATE	PORTION OF THE WEEK	CITATION
	August 24	Ki Thavo	Deuteronomy 26:1–29:8
	August 31*	Netzavim	Deuteronomy 29:9–30:20
	August 31	VaYelekh	Deuteronomy 31:1–31:30
	September 14	HaAzinu	Deuteronomy 32:1–32:52
	September 29†	VeZoth HaBerakhah	Deuteronomy 33:1–34:12
	October 5	Bereshith	Genesis 1:1–6:8
	October 12	Noah	Genesis 6:9–11:32
	October 19	Lekh Lekha	Genesis 12:1–17:27
	October 26	VaYera	Genesis 18:1–22:24
	November 2	Chayay Sarah	Genesis 23:1–25:18
	November 9	Toledoth	Genesis 25:19–28:9
	November 16	VaYetze	Genesis 28:10–32:3
	November 23	VaYishlach	Genesis 32:4–36:43
	November 30	VaYeshev	Genesis 37:1–40:23
	December 7	MiKetz	Genesis 41:1–44:17
	December 14	VaYigash	Genesis 44:18–47:27
	December 21	VaYechi	Genesis 47:28–50:26
	December 28	Shemoth	Exodus 1:1–6:1
2003	January 4	VaEra	Exodus 6:2–9:35
	January 11	Bo	Exodus 10:1–13:16
	January 18	BeShalach	Exodus 13:17–17:16
	January 25	Yithro	Exodus 18:1–20:23
	February 1	Mishpatim	Exodus 21:1–24:18
	February 8	Terumah	Exodus 25:1–27:19
	February 15	Tetzaveh	Exodus 27:20–30:10

*Two Torah portions are combined on the same Shabbat.
†The final chapter of the Torah is read on Simchat Torah, which may occur other than on a Shabbat.

SHABBAT DATE	PORTION OF THE WEEK	CITATION
February 22	Ki Thisa	Exodus 30:11–34:35
March 1	VaYakhel	Exodus 35:1–38:20
March 8	Pekudey	Exodus 38:21–40:38
March 15	VaYikra	Leviticus 1:1–5:26
March 22	Tzav	Leviticus 6:1–8:36
March 29	Shemini	Leviticus 9:1–11:47
April 5	Tazria	Leviticus 12:1–13:59
April 12	Metzorah	Leviticus 14:1–15:33
April 26	Acharey Moth	Leviticus 16:1–18:30
May 3	Kedoshim	Leviticus 19:1–20:27
May 10	Emor	Leviticus 21:1–24:23
May 17	BeHar	Leviticus 25:1–26:2
May 24	BeChuko-thai	Leviticus 26:3–27:34
May 31	BeMidbar	Numbers 1:1–4:20
June 14	Naso	Numbers 4:21–7:89
June 21	BeHa'alothekha	Numbers 8:1–12:16
June 28	Sh'lach	Numbers 13:1–15:41
July 5	Korach	Numbers 16:1–18:32
July 12*	Chukath	Numbers 19:1–22:1
July 12	Balak	Numbers 22:2–25:9
July 19	Pinchas	Numbers 25:10–30:1
July 26*	Mattoth	Numbers 30:2–32:42
July 26	Massey	Numbers 33:1–36:13
August 2	Devarim	Deuteronomy 1:1–3:22
August 9	VeEthChanan	Deuteronomy 3:23–7:11
August 16	Ekev	Deuteronomy 7:12–11:25

*Two Torah portions are combined on the same Shabbat.

	SHABBAT DATE	PORTION OF THE WEEK	CITATION
	August 23	Re'eh	Deuteronomy 11:26–16:17
	August 30	Shof'tim	Deuteronomy 16:18–21:9
	September 6	Ki Thetze	Deuteronomy 21:10–25:18
	September 13	Ki Thavo	Deuteronomy 26:1–29:8
	September 20*	Netzavim	Deuteronomy 29:9–30:20
	September 20	VaYelekh	Deuteronomy 31:1–31:30
	October 4	HaAzinu	Deuteronomy 32:1–32:52
	October 19†	VeZoth HaBerakhah	Deuteronomy 33:1–34:12
	October 25	Bereshith	Genesis 1:1–6:8
	November 1	Noah	Genesis 6:9–11:32
	November 8	Lekh Lekha	Genesis 12:1–17:27
	November 15	VaYera	Genesis 18:1–22:24
	November 22	Chayay Sarah	Genesis 23:1–25:18
	November 29	Toledoth	Genesis 25:19–28:9
	December 6	VaYetze	Genesis 28:10–32:3
	December 13	VaYishlach	Genesis 32:4–36:43
	December 20	VaYeshev	Genesis 37:1–40:23
	December 27	MiKetz	Genesis 41:1–44:17
2004	January 3	VaYigash	Genesis 44:18–47:27
	January 10	VaYechi	Genesis 47:28–50:26
	January 17	Shemoth	Exodus 1:1–6:1
	January 24	VaEra	Exodus 6:2–9:35
	January 31	Bo	Exodus 10:1–13:16
	February 7	BeShalach	Exodus 13:17–17:16
	February 14	Yithro	Exodus 18:1–20:23

*Two Torah portions are combined on the same Shabbat.
†The final chapter of the Torah is read on Simchat Torah, which may occur other than on a Shabbat.

SHABBAT DATE	PORTION OF THE WEEK	CITATION
February 21	Mishpatim	Exodus 21:1–24:18
February 28	Terumah	Exodus 25:1–27:19
March 6	Tetzaveh	Exodus 27:20–30:10
March 13	Ki Thisa	Exodus 30:11–34:35
March 20*	VaYakhel	Exodus 35:1–38:20
March 20	Pekudey	Exodus 38:21–40:38
March 27	VaYikra	Leviticus 1:1–5:26
April 3	Tzav	Leviticus 6:1–8:36
April 17	Shemini	Leviticus 9:1–11:47
April 24*	Tazria	Leviticus 12:1–13:59
April 24	Metzorah	Leviticus 14:1–15:33
May 1*	Acharey Moth	Leviticus 16:1–18:30
May 1	Kedoshim	Leviticus 19:1–20:27
May 8	Emor	Leviticus 21:1–24:23
May 15*	BeHar	Leviticus 25:1–26:2
May 15	BeChuko-thai	Leviticus 26:3–27:34
May 22	BeMidbar	Numbers 1:1–4:20
May 29	Naso	Numbers 4:21–7:89
June 5	BeHa'alothekha	Numbers 8:1–12:16
June 12	Sh'lach	Numbers 13:1–15:41
June 19	Korach	Numbers 16:1–18:32
June 26	Chukath	Numbers 19:1–22:1
July 3	Balak	Numbers 22:2–25:9
July 10	Pinchas	Numbers 25:10–30:1
July 17*	Mattoth	Numbers 30:2–32:42
July 17	Massey	Numbers 33:1–36:13

*Two Torah portions are combined on the same Shabbat.

	SHABBAT DATE	PORTION OF THE WEEK	CITATION
	July 24	Devarim	Deuteronomy 1:1–3:22
	July 31	VeEthChanan	Deuteronomy 3:23–7:11
	August 7	Ekev	Deuteronomy 7:12–11:25
	August 14	Re'eh	Deuteronomy 11:26–16:17
	August 21	Shof'tim	Deuteronomy 16:18–21:9
	August 28	Ki Thetze	Deuteronomy 21:10–25:18
	September 4	Ki Thavo	Deuteronomy 26:1–29:8
	September 11*	Netzavim	Deuteronomy 29:9–30:20
	September 11	VaYelekh	Deuteronomy 31:1–31:30
	September 18	HaAzinu	Deuteronomy 32:1–32:52
	October 8†	VeZoth HaBerakhah	Deuteronomy 33:1–34:12
	October 9	Bereshith	Genesis 1:1–6:8
	October 16	Noah	Genesis 6:9–11:32
	October 23	Lekh Lekha	Genesis 12:1–17:27
	October 30	VaYera	Genesis 18:1–22:24
	November 6	Chayay Sarah	Genesis 23:1–25:18
	November 13	Toledoth	Genesis 25:19–28:9
	November 20	VaYetze	Genesis 28:10–32:3
	November 27	VaYishlach	Genesis 32:4–36:43
	December 4	VaYeshev	Genesis 37:1–40:23
	December 11	MiKetz	Genesis 41:1–44:17
	December 18	VaYigash	Genesis 44:18–47:27
	December 25	VaYechi	Genesis 47:28–50:26
2005	January 1	Shemoth	Exodus 1:1–6:1
	January 8	VaEra	Exodus 6:2–9:35

*Two Torah portions are combined on the same Shabbat.
†The final chapter of the Torah is read on Simchat Torah, which may occur other than on a Shabbat.

	SHABBAT DATE	PORTION OF THE WEEK	CITATION
	January 15	Bo	Exodus 10:1–13:16
	January 22	BeShalach	Exodus 13:17–17:16
	January 29	Yithro	Exodus 18:1–20:23
	February 5	Mishpatim	Exodus 21:1–24:18
	February 12	Terumah	Exodus 25:1–27:19
	February 19	Tetzaveh	Exodus 27:20–30:10
	February 26	Ki Thisa	Exodus 30:11–34:35
	March 5	VaYakhel	Exodus 35:1–38:20
	March 12	Pekudey	Exodus 38:21–40:38
	March 19	VaYikra	Leviticus 1:1–5:26
	March 26	Tzav	Leviticus 6:1–8:36
	April 2	Shemini	Leviticus 9:1–11:47
	April 9	Tazria	Leviticus 12:1–13:59
	April 16	Metzorah	Leviticus 14:1–15:33
	April 23	Acharey Moth	Leviticus 16:1–18:30
	May 7	Kedoshim	Leviticus 19:1–20:27
	May 14	Emor	Leviticus 21:1–24:23
	May 21	BeHar	Leviticus 25:1–26:2
	May 28	BeChuko-thai	Leviticus 26:3–27:34
	June 4	BeMidbar	Numbers 1:1–4:20
	June 11	Naso	Numbers 4:21–7:89
	June 18	BeHa'alothekha	Numbers 8:1–12:16
	June 25	Sh'lach	Numbers 13:1–15:41
	July 2	Korach	Numbers 16:1–18:32
	July 9	Chukath	Numbers 19:1–22:1
	July 16	Balak	Numbers 22:2–25:9
	July 23	Pinchas	Numbers 25:10–30:1

	SHABBAT DATE	PORTION OF THE WEEK	CITATION
	July 30	Mattoth	Numbers 30:2–32:42
	August 6	Massey	Numbers 33:1–36:13
	August 13	Devarim	Deuteronomy 1:1–3:22
	August 20	VeEthChanan	Deuteronomy 3:23–7:11
	August 27	Ekev	Deuteronomy 7:12–11:25
	September 3	Re'eh	Deuteronomy 11:26–16:17
	September 10	Shof'tim	Deuteronomy 16:18–21:9
	September 17	Ki Thetze	Deuteronomy 21:10–25:18
	September 24	Ki Thavo	Deuteronomy 26:1–29:8
	October 1	Netzavim	Deuteronomy 29:9–30:20
	October 8	VaYelekh	Deuteronomy 31:1–31:30
	October 15	HaAzinu	Deuteronomy 32:1–32:52
	October 26[†]	VeZoth HaBerakhah	Deuteronomy 33:1–34:12
	October 29	Bereshith	Genesis 1:1–6:8
	November 5	Noah	Genesis 6:9–11:32
	November 12	Lekh Lekha	Genesis 12:1–17:27
	November 19	VaYera	Genesis 18:1–22:24
	November 26	Chayay Sarah	Genesis 23:1–25:18
	December 3	Toledoth	Genesis 25:19–28:9
	December 10	VaYetze	Genesis 28:10–32:3
	December 17	VaYishlach	Genesis 32:4–36:43
	December 24	VaYeshev	Genesis 37:1–40:23
	December 31	MiKetz	Genesis 41:1–44:17
2006	January 7	VaYigash	Genesis 44:18–47:27
	January 14	VaYechi	Genesis 47:28–50:26
	January 21	Shemoth	Exodus 1:1–6:1

[†]The final chapter of the Torah is read on Simchat Torah, which may occur other than on a Shabbat.

SHABBAT DATE	PORTION OF THE WEEK	CITATION
January 28	VaEra	Exodus 6:2–9:35
February 4	Bo	Exodus 10:1–13:16
February 11	BeShalach	Exodus 13:17–17:16
February 18	Yithro	Exodus 18:1–20:23
February 25	Mishpatim	Exodus 21:1–24:18
March 4	Terumah	Exodus 25:1–27:19
March 11	Tetzaveh	Exodus 27:20–30:10
March 18	Ki Thisa	Exodus 30:11–34:35
March 25*	VaYakhel	Exodus 35:1–38:20
March 25	Pekudey	Exodus 38:21–40:38
April 1	VaYikra	Leviticus 1:1–5:26
April 8	Tzav	Leviticus 6:1–8:36
April 22	Shemini	Leviticus 9:1–11:47
April 29*	Tazria	Leviticus 12:1–13:59
April 29	Metzorah	Leviticus 14:1–15:33
May 6*	Acharey Moth	Leviticus 16:1–18:30
May 6	Kedoshim	Leviticus 19:1–20:27
May 13	Emor	Leviticus 21:1–24:23
May 20*	BeHar	Leviticus 25:1–26:2
May 20	BeChuko-thai	Leviticus 26:3–27:34
May 27	BeMidbar	Numbers 1:1–4:20
June 10	Naso	Numbers 4:21–7:89
June 17	BeHa'alothekha	Numbers 8:1–12:16
June 24	Sh'lach	Numbers 13:1–15:41
July 1	Korach	Numbers 16:1–18:32
July 8*	Chukath	Numbers 19:1–22:1

*Two Torah portions are combined on the same Shabbat.

	SHABBAT DATE	PORTION OF THE WEEK	CITATION
	July 8	Balak	Numbers 22:2–25:9
	July 15	Pinchas	Numbers 25:10–30:1
	July 22*	Mattoth	Numbers 30:2–32:42
	July 22	Massey	Numbers 33:1–36:13
	July 29	Devarim	Deuteronomy 1:1–3:22
	August 5	VeEthChanan	Deuteronomy 3:23–7:11
	August 12	Ekev	Deuteronomy 7:12–11:25
	August 19	Re'eh	Deuteronomy 11:26–16:17
	August 26	Shof'tim	Deuteronomy 16:18–21:9
	September 2	Ki Thetze	Deuteronomy 21:10–25:18
	September 9	Ki Thavo	Deuteronomy 26:1–29:8
	September 16*	Netzavim	Deuteronomy 29:9–30:20
	September 16	VaYelekh	Deuteronomy 31:1–31:30
	September 30	HaAzinu	Deuteronomy 32:1–32:52
	October 15†	VeZoth HaBerakhah	Deuteronomy 33:1–34:12
	October 21	Bereshith	Genesis 1:1–6:8
	October 28	Noah	Genesis 6:9–11:32
	November 4	Lekh Lekha	Genesis 12:1–17:27
	November 11	VaYera	Genesis 18:1–22:24
	November 18	Chayay Sarah	Genesis 23:1–25:18
	November 25	Toledoth	Genesis 25:19–28:9
	December 2	VaYetze	Genesis 28:10–32:3
	December 9	VaYishlach	Genesis 32:4–36:43
	December 16	VaYeshev	Genesis 37:1–40:23
	December 23	MiKetz	Genesis 41:1–44:17
	December 30	VaYigash	Genesis 44:18–47:27

*Two Torah portions are combined on the same Shabbat.
†The final chapter of the Torah is read on Simchat Torah, which may occur other than on a Shabbat.

Index of Torah References

CITATION	PORTION OF THE WEEK	REFER TO PAGE
Genesis 1:1–6:8	Bereshith	7, 29, 30, 31, 79, 83, 92, 110
Genesis 6:9–11:32	Noah	101
Genesis 12:1–17:27	Lekh Lekha	20, 28, 29, 96
Genesis 18:1–22:24	VaYera	17, 31, 32, 33, 59, 84, 85, 101, 102
Genesis 23:1–25:18	Chayay Sarah	97
Genesis 25:19–28:9	Toledoth	31, 82
Genesis 28:10–32:3	VaYetze	31, 94, 102
Genesis 32:4–36:43	VaYishlach	31
Genesis 37:1–40:23	VaYeshev	31, 100
Genesis 41:1–44:17	MiKetz	93, 100
Genesis 44:18–47:27	VaYigash	
Genesis 47:28–50:26	VaYechi	102
Exodus 1:1–6:1	Shemoth	7, 90, 97
Exodus 6:2–9:35	VaEra	70, 91, 93
Exodus 10:1–13:16	Bo	92, 93
Exodus 13:17–17:16	BeShalach	90, 91, 111
Exodus 18:1–20:23	Yithro	95
Exodus 21:1–24:18	Mishpatim	3, 73
Exodus 25:1–27:19	Terumah	11, 104
Exodus 27:20–30:10	Tetzaveh	

CITATION	PORTION OF THE WEEK	REFER TO PAGE
Exodus 30:11– 34:35	Ki Thisa	17, 83, 86, 102
Exodus 35:1– 38:20	VaYakhel	103, 104
Exodus 38:21– 40:38	Pekudey	
Leviticus 1:1– 5:26	VaYikra	7, 113
Leviticus 6:1– 8:36	Tzav	
Leviticus 9:1– 11:47	Shemini	101
Leviticus 12:1– 13:59	Tazria	
Leviticus 14:1– 15:33	Metzorah	
Leviticus 16:1– 18:30	Acharey Moth	
Leviticus 19:1– 20:27	Kedoshin	
Leviticus 21:1– 24:23	Emor	
Leviticus 25:1– 26:2	BeHar	
Leviticus 26:3– 27:34	BeChuko-thai	
Numbers 1:1– 4:20	BeMidbar	7
Numbers 4:21– 7:89	Naso	
Numbers 8:1– 12:16	BeHa'alothekha	
Numbers 13:1– 15:41	Sh'lach	89
Numbers 16:1– 18:32	Korach	98
Numbers 19:1– 22:1	Chukath	26, 87, 88
Numbers 22:2– 25:9	Balak	88
Numbers 25:10– 30:1	Pinchas	25, 66
Numbers 30:2– 32:42	Mattoth	
Numbers 33:1– 36:13	Massey	66, 67
Deuteronomy 1:1– 3:22	Devarim	7
Deuteronomy 3:23– 7:11	VeEthChanan	
Deuteronomy 7:12– 11:25	Ekev	
Deuteronomy 11:26– 16:17	Re'eh	101